TEACHER'S PET PUBLICATIONS

LITPLAN TEACHER PACK
for
Hiroshima
based on the book by
John Hersey

Written by
Mary B. Collins

© 1996 Teacher's Pet Publications
All Rights Reserved

This **LitPlan** for John Hersey's
Hiroshima
has been brought to you by Teacher's Pet Publications, Inc.

Copyright Teacher's Pet Publications 1996
11504 Hammock Point
Berlin MD 21811

Only the student materials in this unit plan (such as worksheets,
study questions, and tests) may be reproduced multiple times
for use in the purchaser's classroom.

For any additional copyright questions,
contact Teacher's Pet Publications.

www.tpet.com

TABLE OF CONTENTS - *Hiroshima*

Introduction	5
Unit Objectives	7
Reading Assignment Sheet	8
Unit Outline	9
Study Questions (Short Answer)	13
Quiz/Study Questions (Multiple Choice)	18
Pre-reading Vocabulary Worksheets	29
Lesson One (Introductory Lesson)	43
Nonfiction Assignment Sheet	46
Oral Reading Evaluation Form	47
Writing Assignment 1	58
Writing Assignment 2	64
Writing Assignment 3	66
Writing Evaluation Form	67
Vocabulary Review Activities	61
Extra Writing Assignments/Discussion ?s	60
Unit Review Activities	68
Unit Tests	71
Unit Resource Materials	103
Vocabulary Resource Materials	119

A FEW NOTES ABOUT THE AUTHOR
John Hersey

HERSEY, JOHN (1914-93), U.S. writer, born on June 17, 1914, in Tianjin, China. His works combined his reporting skills with personal sensitivity and social concern. Hersey wrote a wide variety of fiction and nonfiction ranging from a study of survivors of World War II atrocities to futuristic musings to a novel consisting of letters written between the ancient poets of Seneca and Lucan.

As a child, Hersey lived in China while his mother worked as a missionary and his father worked as a secretary for the Young Men's Christian Association. They returned to America when John was 10 years old, and he later studied at Yale University, from which he graduated in 1936. He then worked for Life and Time magazines and served as a war correspondent during World War II.

Hersey's early works included 'Men on Bataan' (1942) and 'Into the Valley' (1943). His widely praised book 'Hiroshima' (1946), which was first published in *The New Yorker*, was an account of the effects of the 1945 atomic bomb explosion over Hiroshima, Japan, on six survivors of the attack. Hersey's novels included 'A Bell for Adano' (1944), which won the Pulitzer prize for fiction in 1945 and was dramatized on stage and screen; 'The Wall' (1950), which told the story of Jewish resistance in the Warsaw ghetto from 1939 to 1943; and 'The Child Buyer' (1960). His other books included 'The Algiers Motel Incident' (1968), 'The Conspiracy' (1972), 'My Petition for More Space' (1974), and 'The Call' (1985). Several of his works, including 'The Child Buyer', 'The War Lover', and 'The Wall', were adapted for the theater and as motion pictures.

Hersey lectured at Yale and the Massachusetts Institute of Technology, and he received honorary degrees from several colleges and universities, including yale, Washington and Jefferson College, and Wesleyan University. He died on March 24, 1993, in Key West, Florida.

----- Courtesy of Compton's Learning Company

INTRODUCTION - *Hiroshima*

This unit has been designed to develop students' reading, writing, thinking, and language skills through exercises and activities related to *Hiroshima* by John Fitzgerald. It includes twenty lessons, supported by extra resource materials.

The **introductory lesson** introduces students to some background to the novel through a guest speaker. Following the introductory activity, students are given a transition to explain how the activity relates to the book they are about to read.

The **reading assignments** are approximately thirty pages each; some are a little shorter while others are a little longer. Students have approximately 15 minutes of pre-reading work to do prior to each reading assignment. This pre-reading work involves reviewing the study questions for the assignment and doing some vocabulary work for 8 to 10 vocabulary words they will encounter in their reading.

The **study guide questions** are fact-based questions; students can find the answers to these questions right in the text. These questions come in two formats: short answer or multiple choice. The best use of these materials is probably to use the short answer version of the questions as study guides for students (since answers will be more complete), and to use the multiple choice version for occasional quizzes. It might be a good idea to make transparencies of your answer keys for the overhead projector.

The **vocabulary work** is intended to enrich students' vocabularies as well as to aid in the students' understanding of the book. Prior to each reading assignment, students will complete a two-part worksheet for approximately 8 to 10 vocabulary words in the upcoming reading assignment. Part I focuses on students' use of general knowledge and contextual clues by giving the sentence in which the word appears in the text. Students are then to write down what they think the words mean based on the words' usage. Part II nails down the definitions of the words by giving students dictionary definitions of the words and having students match the words to the correct definitions based on the words' contextual usage. Students should then have an understanding of the words when they meet them in the text.

After each reading assignment, students will go back and formulate answers for the study guide questions. Discussion of these questions serves as a **review** of the most important events and ideas presented in the reading assignments.

After students complete reading the work, there is a **vocabulary review** lesson which pulls together all of the fragmented vocabulary lists for the reading assignments and gives students a review of all of the words they have studied.

A lesson is devoted to the **extra discussion questions/writing assignments**. These questions focus on interpretation, critical analysis and personal response, employing a variety of thinking skills and adding to the students' understanding of the novel.

There is a **group activity** in which students work in small groups to put the events in the lives of each of the survivors into chronological order.

There are three **writing assignments** in this unit, each with the purpose of informing, persuading, or having students express personal opinions. The first assignment is to inform: students create the narrative script for their video tape segments (related to a **research project**). The second assignment is to persuade: students take a stance regarding the dropping of the bomb on Hiroshima and then attempt to persuade someone from the opposite viewpoint that theirs is the right view. The third assignment is to give students a chance to express their own opinions about the role of Japan in the world in the next fifty years.

In addition, there is a **nonfiction reading assignment**. Students are required to read a piece of nonfiction related in some way to *Hiroshima*. After reading their nonfiction pieces, students will fill out a worksheet on which they answer questions regarding facts, interpretation, criticism, and personal opinions. This nonfiction reading assignment is done in conjunction with the research project in which students are each assigned specific topics about Japan to research. After the research is done, students have to create a five minute video taped segment in which they summarize the information they have found in a narration to relevant visuals (also found and planned by the students).

The **review lesson** pulls together all of the aspects of the unit. The teacher is given four or five choices of activities or games to use which all serve the same basic function of reviewing all of the information presented in the unit.

The **unit test** comes in two formats: multiple choice or short answer. As a convenience, two different tests for each format have been included. There is also an advanced short answer test for students who need more of a challenge.

There are additional **support materials** included with this unit. The **unit resources** section includes suggestions for an in-class library, crossword and word search puzzles related to the novel, and extra vocabulary worksheets. There is a list of **bulletin board ideas** which gives the teacher suggestions for bulletin boards to go along with this unit. In addition, there is a list of **extra class activities** the teacher could choose from to enhance the unit or as a substitution for an exercise the teacher might feel is inappropriate for his/her class. **Answer keys** are located directly after the **reproducible student materials** throughout the unit. The student materials may be reproduced for use in the teacher's classroom without infringement of copyrights. No other portion of this unit may be reproduced without the written consent of Teacher's Pet Publications, Inc.

UNIT OBJECTIVES - *Hiroshima*

1. Students will learn about an important part of U.S. and world history.

2. Students will demonstrate their understanding of the text on four levels: factual, interpretive, critical and personal.

3. Students will consider and study the cause and effect relationship of how one event can have multiple consequences.

4. Students will study point of view.

5. Students will be given the opportunity to practice reading aloud and silently to improve their skills in each area.

6. Students will answer questions to demonstrate their knowledge and understanding of the main events and characters in *Hiroshima* as they relate to the author's theme development.

7. Students will enrich their vocabularies and improve their understanding of the novel through the vocabulary lessons prepared for use in conjunction with the novel.

8. The writing assignments in this unit are geared to several purposes:
    a. To have students demonstrate their abilities to inform, to persuade, or to express their own personal ideas
    Note: Students will demonstrate ability to write effectively to <u>inform</u> by developing and organizing facts to convey information. Students will demonstrate the ability to write effectively to <u>persuade</u> by selecting and organizing relevant information, establishing an argumentative purpose, and by designing an appropriate strategy for an identified audience. Students will demonstrate the ability to write effectively to <u>express personal ideas</u> by selecting a form and its appropriate elements.
    b. To check the students' reading comprehension
    c. To make students think about the ideas presented by the novel
    d. To encourage logical thinking
    e. To provide an opportunity to practice good grammar and improve students' use of the English language.

READING ASSIGNMENT SHEET - *Hiroshima*

Date Assigned	Assignment	Completion Date
	Part One	
	Part Two	
	Part Three	
	Part Four	
	Part Five	

UNIT OUTLINE - *Hiroshima*

1 Speaker	2 PVR 1	3 Study ?s 1 PVR 2	4 Study ?s 2 Point of View Assignment	5 Writing Assignment #1 PVR 3
6 Study ?s 3 Point of View Conclusion	7 PVR 4	8 Study ?s 4 Japan Assignment	9 PVR 5	10 Study ?s 5 Extra ?s
11 Vocabulary	12 Japan Assignment Working Session	13 Group Activity Chronology	14 Writing Assignment #2	15 Japan
16 Japan	17 Film	18 Writing Assignment #3	19 Review	20 Test

Key: P=Preview Study Questions V=Vocabulary Worksheets R=Read

STUDY GUIDE QUESTIONS

SHORT ANSWER STUDY GUIDE QUESTIONS - *Hiroshima*

One
1. On what date, at what time, and where was the first atomic bomb set off?
2. Identify the six survivors about whom the book is written.
3. Describe the geographical situation of Hiroshima at the time the bomb was dropped.
4. Why did the atomic bomb take the Japanese by surprise? Why were they not expecting it?
5. What was unusual about the way the bomb affected the people at the time of its explosion?

Two
1. Mr. Tanimoto, like the other survivors, was amazed when he looked out over the city after the bomb. Why?
2. Identify Asano Park.
3. The condition of Fr. Kleinsorge's room after the bomb was fairly typical of the bizarre effect of the bomb. Describe his room.
4. What explanation did Dr. Machii give for the destruction?
5. At first there were very few fires. Why were so many people burned?
6. Why were so many citizens who were hurt unattended by doctors and nurses?
7. What were the estimated casualties just after the bomb hit?
8. What was unusual about Mr. Tanimoto's meeting with his wife?
9. Why did the people go to the park and to the river?
10. Why were the people nauseated?
11. Why did many people die in the river?

Three
1. Why did Mr. Tanimoto have to keep reminding himself, "These are human beings"?
2. The doctor at the East Parade Ground said his first duty was to take care of the slightly wounded. Why?
3. What happened at two minutes after eleven o'clock on the morning of August 9th?

Four
1. When Miss Sasaki saw the ruins of Hiroshima for the first time, what gave her the creeps?
2. A few weeks to a month after the bomb, what symptoms were people having?
3. On September 17th, another disaster happened at Hiroshima. What was it?
4. Why was Mrs. Nakamura's sewing machine important? What happened to it?
5. Why was Fr. Kleinsorge weak, pale and shaky?
6. What disease of the blood was becoming common among survivors?
7. What were the three stages of radiation sickness?
8. What was the population of Hiroshima by November 1st?
9. Approximately what was the temperature of the center of the bomb's "explosion"?

Five
1. What were the survivors called? What did the name mean? Why was it chosen?
2. Why did the hibakusha suffer for more than a decade after the bombings?

ANSWER KEY: SHORT ANSWER STUDY GUIDE QUESTIONS - *Hiroshima*

One

1. On what date, at what time, and where was the first atomic bomb set off?
    It was set off at fifteen minutes past eight in the morning on August 6, 1945 over the city of Hiroshima, Japan.

2. Identify the six survivors about whom the book is written.
    Miss Toshinki Sasaki, Dr. Masakazu Fujii, Mrs. Hatsuyo Nakamura, Fr. Wilhelm Kleinsorge, Dr. Terufumi Sasaki, and The Reverend Mister Kiyoshi Tanimoto

3. Describe the geographical situation of Hiroshima at the time the bomb was dropped.
    "Hiroshima was a fan-shaped city, lying mostly on the six islands formed by the seven estuarial rivers that branch out from the Ota River; its main commercial and residential districts, covering about four square miles in the center of the city, contained three-quarters of its population, which had been reduced by several evacuation programs from a wartime peak of 380,000 to about 245,000. Factories and other residential districts, or suburbs, lay compactly around the city. To the south were the docks, an airport, and the island-studded Inland Sea. A rim of mountains runs around the other three sides of the delta.

4. Why did the atomic bomb take the Japanese by surprise? Why were they not expecting it?
    The warning siren went off at seven and the people went to their "safe areas." At eight o'clock, the all clear siren sounded. Because the atomic bomb was dropped by a single plane, the plane was not seen as a threat, and no warning siren was given. So at 8:15 when the bomb was dropped, the citizens of Hiroshima were totally off-guard.

5. What was unusual about the way the bomb affected the people at the time of its explosion?
    The people saw a bright light and then were suddenly picked up and moved by a great, unseen force. There was no noise of explosion following the bomb. There was a huge dust cloud which the people thought was just in their local areas and which made the day grow dark.

Two

1. Mr. Tanimoto, like the other survivors, was amazed when he looked out over the city after the bomb. Why?
    "Not just a patch of Koi, as he had expected, but as much of Hiroshima as he could see through the clouded air was giving off a thick, dreadful miasma. . . . He wondered how such extensive damage could have been dealt out of a silent sky."

2. Identify Asano Park.
    It was an estate by the Kyo River which had been designated as an evacuation area.

3. The condition of Fr. Kleinsorge's room after the bomb was fairly typical of the bizarre effect of the bomb. Describe his room.

   "A first-aid kit was hanging undisturbed on a hook on the wall, but his clothes, which had been on other hooks nearby, were nowhere to be seen. His desk was in splinters all over the room, but a mere papier-mache suitcase, which he had hidden under the desk, stood handle-side up, without a scratch on it, in the doorway of the room, where he could not miss it.

4. What explanation did Dr. Machii give for the destruction?

   He thought it was a Molotov flower basket, a self-scattering cluster of bombs.

5. At first there were very few fires. Why were so many people burned?

   The people suffered radiation burns.

6. Why were so many citizens who were hurt unattended by doctors and nurses?

   "Of a hundred and fifty doctors in the city, sixty-five were already dead, and most of the rest were wounded. Of 1,780 nurses, 1,654 were dead or too badly hurt to work."

7. What were the estimated casualties just after the bomb hit?

   "In a city of 245,000, nearly a hundred thousand people had been killed or doomed at one blow; a hundred thousand more were hurt."

8. What was unusual about Mr. Tanimoto's meeting with his wife?

   "Mr. Tanimoto was now so emotionally worn out that nothing could surprise him. He did not embrace his wife; he simply said, 'Oh, you are safe.' . . . They parted as casually -- as bewildered as they had met."

9. Why did the people go to the park and to the river?

   The park was designated as a safe area, it had not been destroyed by the bomb, and they thought that if the Americans would return, they would only bomb buildings. They went to the river to escape the fires which the winds were blowing out of control, and the people were thirsty and drank from the river.

10. Why were the people nauseated?

    They felt they were sick from the gas the Americans had dropped, but actually they had radiation sickness and were ill also from drinking brackish water.

11. Why did many people die in the river?

    Frightened people in the park pushed closer to the river to escape the raging fires, and the people who were on the banks of the river were pushed in by the mob.

Three
1. Why did Mr. Tanimoto have to keep reminding himself, "These are human beings"?
    "[He] lifted several of the men and women, who were naked, into his boat. Their backs and breasts were clammy, and he remembered uneasily what the great burns he had seen during the day had been like: yellow at first, then red and swollen, with the skin sloughed off, and finally, in the evening, suppurated and smelly. . . . He lifted the slimy living bodies out and carried them up the slope away from the tide."

2. The doctor at the East Parade Ground said his first duty was to take care of the slightly wounded. Why?
    "In an emergency like this, the first task is to help as many as possible -- to save as many lives as possible. There is no hope for the heavily wounded. They will die. We can't bother with them."

3. What happened at two minutes after eleven o'clock on the morning of August 9th?
    The second atomic bomb was dropped on Nagasaki.

Four
1. When Miss Sasaki saw the ruins of Hiroshima for the first time, what gave her the creeps?
    "Over everything -- up through the wreckage of the city, in gutters, along the river banks, tangled among tiles and tin roofing, climbing on charred tree trunks -- was a blanket of fresh, vivid, lush, optimistic green; the verdancy rose even from the foundations of ruined houses. Weeds already hid the ashes, and wild flowers were in bloom among the city's bones."

2. A few weeks to a month after the bomb, what symptoms were people having?
    Some people had a feeling of extreme weakness, of being tired. Others were beginning to have spot hemorrhages. Many people were losing their hair.

3. On September 17th, another disaster happened at Hiroshima. What was it?
    There was a cloud burst and then a typhoon. The flood took up where the bomb left off and caused more destruction.

4. Why was Mrs. Nakamura's sewing machine important? What happened to it?
    She submerged it in her water well on the morning the bomb went off, in an effort to keep it safe, because it was her means of livelihood. When it was pulled up again, it was rusted and useless, leaving her poor and in need of a way to make a living.

5. Why was Fr. Kleinsorge weak, pale and shaky?
    His white blood count was very low.

6. What disease of the blood was becoming common among survivors?
    Leukemia was becoming common.

7. What were the three stages of radiation sickness?

> Stage one occurred at the moment when the bomb went off. Apparently uninjured people died due to overdoses of radiation. "The rays simply destroyed body cells -- caused their nuclei to degenerate and broke their walls." The second stage set in ten or fifteen days after the bombing. Its symptoms were falling hair, diarrhea, and fever. Also blood disorders appeared in the second stage. White blood cell counts dropped, and small hemorrhages appeared on the skin and mucous membranes. Patients also suffered anemia. In the third stage, the body struggled to compensate for its ills. For instance, the white count not only returned to normal, but increased to much higher than normal levels. Complications also occurred in this stage.

8. What was the population of Hiroshima by November 1st?

> 137,000

9. Approximately what was the temperature of the center of the bomb's "explosion"?

> It was about 6000 degrees C.

<u>Five</u>

1. What were the survivors called? What did the name mean? Why was it chosen?

> ". . . The Japanese tended to shy away from the term 'survivors,' because in its focus on being alive, it might suggest some slight to the sacred dead. The class of people to which the Nakamura-san belonged came, therefore, to be called by a more neutral name, 'hibakusha' – literally, 'explosion-affected persons.'"

2. Why did the hibakusha suffer for more than a decade after the bombings?

> The Japanese government did not want to find itself saddled with anything like moral responsibility for the heinous acts of the victorious United States."

MULTIPLE CHOICE STUDY/QUIZ QUESTIONS - *Hiroshima*

Chapter 1

1. On what date, and at what time, and where was the first atomic bomb set off?
    A. It was set off at half past nine in the evening on July 4, 1944, over the city of Hiroshima, Korea.
    B. It was set off at fifteen minutes past eight in the morning on August 6, 1945, over the city of Hiroshima, Japan.
    C. It was set off at noon on August 23, 1945, over the city of Hiroshima, Viet Nam.
    D. It was set of at noon on August 23, 1945, over the city of Hiroshima, Formosa.

2. Who of the following is not one of the survivors about whom the book is written?
    A. Mrs. Ryoko Menaka Greene, R.N.
    B. Dr. Masakazu Fujii.
    C. Fr. Wilhelm Kleinsorge.
    D. Reverend Mister Kiyoshi Tanimoto.

3. Which of the following statements does not describe the geographical situation of Hiroshima at the time the bomb was dropped?
    A. It was a fan-shaped city, lying mostly on the six islands formed by the seven estuarial rivers that branched out from the Ota Rivers.
    B. The main commercial and residential districts covered four square miles.
    C. The population was 385,000.
    D. A rim of mountains ran around three sides of the delta, with the docks and the airport and the sea to the south.

4. Why did the atomic bomb take the inhabitants by surprise?
    A. They had been told the war was over.
    B. No one believed the United States had the scientific capability of building such a bomb.
    C. There had been so many recent scares and warning sirens that the people were starting to ignore them.
    D. Only one plane was see in the sky, and it was not thought of as dangerous.

5. True or False: The people first heard a loud explosion and then saw a huge dust cloud. The cloud cleared, they saw a bright light.
    A. True
    B. False

Hiroshima Multiple Choice Study/Quiz Questions Page 2

Chapter 2

6. The survivors were amazed when they looked out over the city after the bomb. Why?
    A. The entire city was on fire.
    B. There were no buildings standing.
    C. Much of the city was giving off a thick, dreadful miasma.
    D. The city was in much better shape physically than anyone had expected it to be.

7. What is Asano Park?
    A. It is an estate by the Kyo River which had been designated as an evacuation area.
    B. It is a stadium that had been used as a field hospital.
    C. It is a wealthy suburb that was relatively unharmed.
    D. It is a playground where many children died.

8. True or False: This statement describes the condition of one of the survivor's rooms after the bomb. "A first-aid kit was hanging undisturbed on a hook on the wall, but his clothes which had been on other hooks nearby, were nowhere to be seen. His desk was in splinters all over the room, but a mere papier-mache suitcase, which he had hidden under the desk, stood handle-up without a scratch on it, in the doorway of the room, where he could not miss it."
    A. True, this statement describes the condition of the room.
    B. False, this statement does not describe the condition of the room.

9. What explanation did Dr. Machii give for the destruction?
    A. He thought it was Agent Orange.
    B. He thought the bomb had also triggered an earthquake.
    C. He thought it was because so many buildings in the city were made of flimsy materials, with shoddy workmanship.
    D. He thought it was a self-scattering cluster of bombs.

10. Why were so many people burned?
    A. They were burned in the severe fires that started immediately after the explosion.
    B. Many people stayed outside to look at the damage, and were sunburned.
    C. They suffered radiation burns.
    D. Many people were cooking over open fires when the bomb was dropped, and had kitchen fires.

Hiroshima Multiple Choice Study/Quiz Questions Page 3

11. Why were so many citizens who were hurt unattended by doctors and nurses?
    A. The government had told the medical personnel to take care of the wounded soldiers first.
    B. Most of the medical personnel were either dead or too wounded to work.
    C. The doctors and nurses had been evacuated during an earlier alarm, and were not in the city when the bombing occurred.
    D. The doctors and nurses had made a pact to take care of their own families first, since supplies were so limited.

12. What were the estimated casualties just after the bomb hit?
    A. Nearly 100,000 had been killed or doomed; 100,000 more were hurt.
    B. Half of the population, or 122,000 were either dead or wounded. The others were safe.
    C. All but 50 people in the city were dead.
    D. 200,000 were hurt, and 50,000 were dead.

13. True or False: When Mr. Tanimoto met his wife, they embraced and held onto each other frantically. They vowed never to part again for one minute.
    A. True
    B. False

14. Where did the people go to be safe?
    A. They went into the underground shelters.
    B. They went to the hospital, which was still standing.
    C. They went to the mountains.
    D. They went to the park and to the river.

15. Why were the people nauseated?
    A. They had radiation sickness, and had been drinking brackish water.
    B. They were sick from the gas the Americans had dropped.
    C. They were hungry and ill from exposure to the elements.
    D. It was fear combined with exhaustion.

16. True or False: Many people died in the river when frightened people in the park pushed closer to the river and the people who were on the banks were pushed in by the mob.
    A. True
    B. False

Hiroshima Multiple Choice Study/Quiz Questions Page 4

Chapter 3

17. One of the survivors was rescuing wounded people, What did he have to keep reminding himself while he did so?
    A. He tried to take the children and the elderly first.
    B. He wanted to help all of the people, regardless of the clan they belonged to.
    C. He was helping human beings.
    D. They were probably contagious, and he should try to keep his nose and mouth covered.

18. Who was the doctor at the East Parade Ground taking care of first?
    A. He was taking care of children and pregnant women, because they had no one else to look after them.
    B. He was taking care of the most seriously injured, to get them to perimeter hospitals and clear the area.
    C. He was taking care of the military personnel, so they could get back to work.
    D. He was taking care of the slightly wounded, in order to save as many lives as possible.

19. What happened at two minutes after eleven o'clock on the morning of August 9th?
    A. Japan retaliated and bombed Pearl Harbor.
    B. The war was officially ended and peace was declared.
    C. The was a huge earthquake that leveled the city and killed most of the bomb survivors.
    D. A second atomic bomb was dropped on Nagasaki.

Hiroshima Multiple Choice Study/Quiz Questions Page 5

Chapter 4

20. When Miss Sasaki saw the ruins of Hiroshima for the first time, what gave her the creeps?
    A. There was a blanket of fresh, lush green, and wild flowers were blooming.
    B. There were skeletons all over the streets, and they were giving off a yellow-green glow.
    C. The city was deathly quiet-there were no sounds of cars, or of children playing.
    D. Everything was dark. There was no electricity, and the sun was hidden by a covering of smoke and ash.

21. A few weeks to a month after the bomb people were having many symptoms. Which of the following is not one of the symptoms?
    A. Feelings of extreme weakness.
    B. A wracking cough.
    C. Loss of hair.
    D. Spot hemorrhages.

22. On September 17th, another disaster happened at Hiroshima. What was it?
    A. There was an epidemic of smallpox.
    B. There was a 7.2 magnitude earthquake.
    C. The people were so scared and frustrated that they began rioting in the streets. Many were killed and injured, and the rioting lasted far into the night.
    D. There was a cloudburst and a typhoon, which caused a flood.

23. Why was Mrs. Nakamura's sewing machine important, and what happened to it?
    A. It was her means of livelihood, so she submerged it in her water well to save it. When it was pulled up, it was rusted and useless.
    B. It was an heirloom that would have brought a good price on the antique market. She was going to sell it and use the money to buy passage to Canada, but it was crushed when a large wardrobe closet fell over on it.
    C. It was a wedding gift from her husband. She had put it in a storage room in their house, since she was no longer using it. Some thieves broke in after the bombing and stole it. Since her husband had been killed, the sewing machine was all she had left to remind her of him. She became very depressed, and was unable to care for herself.
    D. It was a model she had designed herself. She was hoping to be able to obtain a patent, and start to manufacture them. She was keeping it on her sun porch. After the bomb was dropped, the machine and everything else on the porch melted from the intense heat.

Hiroshima Multiple Choice Study/Quiz Questions Page 6

24. Why was Fr. Kleinsorge weak, pale, and shaky?
    A. He had developed dysentery.
    B. It was his nerves. He was having panic attacks about the bombing.
    C. His white blood count was very low.
    D. He wasn't eating enough. There wasn't enough food, so he was feeding his parishioners first.

25. What disease was becoming common among the survivors?
    A. It was tuberculosis.
    B. It was leukemia.
    C. It was meningitis.
    D. It was hyperthyroidism.

26. There were three stages of radiation sickness. True or False: In stage one, people experienced falling hair, diarrhea, and fever.
    A. True
    B. False

27. In which stage did the white cell count increase to higher than normal levels, and complications arise?
    A. Stage one.
    B. Stage two.
    C. Stage three.

28. True or False: The rays of radiation destroyed body cells, caused their nuclei to degenerate and break the walls.
    A. True
    B. False

29. What was the population of Hiroshima by November 1st?
    A. It was 234,000.
    B. It was only 150.
    C. It was 86,000.
    D. It was 137,000.

30. Approximately what was the temperature of the center of the bomb's explosion?
    A. It was 6000 degrees C.
    B. It was 1150 degrees C.
    C. It was 8400 degrees C.
    D. It was 10, 570 degrees C.

Hiroshima Multiple Choice Study/Quiz Questions Page 7

Chapter 5

31. True or False: The survivors were called "hibakusha", which meant "explosion-affected persons," instead of survivors, so they would not dishonor the sacred dead.
    A. True
    B. False

32. Why did the survivors suffer for more than a decade after the bombings?
    A. The entire country was so depressed that no one could figure out what to do.
    B. The government did not want to find itself saddled with anything like moral responsibility for the heinous acts of the victorious United States.
    C. Most of the doctors and nurses had died, and there was no one to work on finding a cure.
    D. The people were trying to show the rest of the world that they regretted the Japanese involvement in the war. They saw their suffering as a means of atonement for the sins of their leaders.

ANSWER KEY - MULTIPLE CHOICE STUDY/QUIZ QUESTIONS
Hiroshima

Chapter 1	Chapter 2	Chapter 3	Chapter 4	Chapter 5
1. B	6. C	17. C	20. A	31. A
2. A	7. A	18. D	21. B	32. B
3. C	8. A	19. C	22. D	
4. D	9. D		23. A	
5. B	10. C		24. C	
	11. B		25. B	
	12. A		26. B	
	13. B		27. C	
	14. D		28. B	
	15. A		29. D	
	16. A		30. A	

PREREADING VOCABULARY WORKSHEETS

VOCABULARY - *Hiroshima*

Chapter One Part I: Using Prior Knowledge and Contextual Clues

Below are the sentences in which the vocabulary words appear in the text. Read the sentence. Use any clues you can find in the sentence combined with your prior knowledge, and write what you think the underlined words mean on the lines provided.

1. Each of them counts many small items of chance or volition—a step taken in time, a decision to go indoors, catching one streetcar instead of the next—that spared him.

2. The Japanese radar operators, detecting only three planes, supposed that they comprised a reconnaissance.

3. He said that she should remain at home unless an urgent warning—a series of intermittent blasts of the siren—was sounded.

4. The prefectural government, convinced, as everyone in Hiroshima was, that the city would be attacked soon, had begun to press with threats and warnings for the completion of wide fire lanes, which, it was hoped might act in conjunction with the rivers to localize any fires started by an incendiary raid.

5. Timbers fell around her as she landed, and a shower of tiles pommeled her; everything became dark, for she was buried.

6. In the days right before the bombing, Dr. Masakazu Fujii, being prosperous, hedonistic, and at the time not too busy, had been allowing himself the luxury of sleeping until nine or nine-thirty, but fortunately he had to get up early the morning the bomb was dropped to see a house guest off on a train.

7. At fifty, he was healthy, convivial, and calm, and he was pleased to pass the evenings drinking whiskey with friends, always sensibly and for the sake of conversation.

8. The Japanese wartime diet had not sustained him, and he felt the strain of being a foreigner in an increasingly xenophobic Japan; even a German, since the defeat of the Fatherland, was unpopular.

Hiroshima Vocabulary Worksheet Chapter One Page 2

9. Satisfied that nothing would happen, he went in and breakfasted with the other Fathers on substitute coffee and ration bread, which, under the circumstances was especially <u>repugnant</u> to him.

_____

Part II: Determining the Meaning -- Match the vocabulary words to their definitions.

____ 1. volition	A. stopping and starting at intervals
____ 2. reconnaissance	B. beat; hit
____ 3. intermittent	C. having a fear of foreigners
____ 4. incendiary	D. conscious decision
____ 5. pommeled	E. characterized by the pursuit of sensual pleasures
____ 6. hedonistic	F. repulsive; disgusting; offensive
____ 7. convivial	G. exploration of an area to get information
____ 8. xenophobic	H. sociable
____ 9. repugnant	I. of or containing chemicals that cause fire when exploded

Hiroshima Vocabulary Worksheet Chapter Two

Part I: Using Prior Knowledge and Contextual Clues

Below are the sentences in which the vocabulary words appear in the text. Read the sentence. Use any clues you can find in the sentence combined with your prior knowledge, and write what you think the underlined words mean on the lines provided.

1. By this solicitous behavior, Mr. Tanimoto at once got rid of his terror.

_____

2. Not just a patch of Koi, as he had expected, but as much of Hiroshima as he could see through the clouded air was giving off a thick, dreadful miasma.

_____

3. While Father LaSalle and Mrs. Murata, the mission housekeeper, dug the teacher out, Father Kleinsorge went to the catechist's fallen house and began lifting things off the top of the pile.

_____

4. Father Kleinsorge later came to regard this as a bit of Providential interference, inasmuch as the suitcase contained his breviary, the account books for the whole diocese, and a considerable amount of paper money belonging to the mission, for which he was responsible.

_____

5. Dr. Fujii went down into the water under the bridge, where a score of people had already taken refuge, among them his servants, who had extricated themselves from the wreckage.

_____

6. Father Kleinsorge, already growing apathetic and dazed in the presence of the cumulative distress, said, "We haven't much time."

_____

7. In a paroxysm of terrified strength, he freed himself and ran down the alleys of Nobori-cho, hemmed in by the fire he had said would never come.

_____

8. This private estate was far enough away from the explosion so that its bamboos, pines, laurel, and maples were still alive and,...because of an irresistible, atavistic urge to hide under leaves.

_____

Hiroshima Vocabulary Worksheet Chapter Two Page 2

Part II: Determining the Meaning -- Match the vocabulary words to their definitions.

    ____ 1. solicitous   A. pulled out
    ____ 2. miasma   B. marked by anxious care and attentiveness
    ____ 3. catechist   C. book containing prayers and hymns
    ____ 4. breviary   D. poisonous atmosphere
    ____ 5. extricated   E. sudden outburst
    ____ 6. apathetic   F. return of a trait after a period of absence
    ____ 7. paroxysm   G. those who teach Christian doctrine
    ____ 8. atavistic   H. uninterested; uncaring

Hiroshima Vocabulary Worksheet Chapter Three

Part I: Using Prior Knowledge and Contextual Clues

Below are the sentences in which the vocabulary words appear in the text. Read the sentence. Use any clues you can find in the sentence combined with your prior knowledge, and write what you think the underlined words mean on the lines provided.

1. ...he remembered uneasily what the great burns he had seen during the day had been like; yellow at first, then red and swollen, with the skin sloughed off, finally, in the evening, suppurated and smelly.

2. By the light of a lantern, he had examined himself and found: extensive contusions on chest and trunk; a couple of ribs possibly fractured.

3. Early that day, August 7th, the Japanese radio broadcast for the first time a succinct announcement that very few, if any, of the people most concerned with its content, the survivors in Hiroshima, happened to hear.

4. Then one of the Jesuits...remembered that they had suffered property damage at the hands of the enemy, they could enter a claim for compensation with the prefectural police.

5. He walked back to the Novitiate, stupefied and without any new understanding.

6. He retrieved some diaries and church records that had been kept in books and were only charred around the edges, as well as some cooking utensils and pottery.

7. He made an incision and put in a rubber pipe to drain off the putrescence.

8. Beginning on the second day, whenever a patient appeared to be moribund, a piece of paper with his name on it was fastened to his clothing.

Hiroshima Vocabulary Worksheet Chapter Three Page 2

Part II: Determining the Meaning--Match the vocabulary words to their definitions.

    ____ 1. suppurated   A. scorched
    ____ 2. contusions   B. district administered or governed by a prefect
    ____ 3. succinct   C. decomposed, rotten, foul-smelling matter
    ____ 4. prefectural   D. with senses dulled by amazement
    ____ 5. stupefied   E. short; to the point
    ____ 6. charred   F. full of pus
    ____ 7. putrescence   G. bruises
    ____ 8. moribund   H. about to die

Hiroshima Vocabulary Worksheet Chapter Four

Part I: Using Prior Knowledge and Contextual Clues

Below are the sentences in which the vocabulary words appear in the text. Read the sentence. Use any clues you can find in the sentence combined with your prior knowledge, and write what you think the underlined words mean on the lines provided.

1. He had begun to think that this bag, in which he kept his valuables, had a talismanic quality, because of the way he had found it after the explosion,...

   _____

2. Now he was using it to carry the yen belonging to the Society of Jesus to the Hiroshima branch of the Yokohama Specie Bank already reopened in its half-ruined building.

   _____

3.-4. By now he was accustomed to the terrible scene through which he walked on his way into the city:... the houses on the outskirts of the city, standing but decrepit, with broken windows and dishevelled tiles;...the beginning of the four square miles of reddish-brown scar, where nearly everything had been buffeted down and burned; range on range of collapsed city locks...

   _____

   _____

5. Mr. Tanimoto fell suddenly ill with a general malaise, weariness, and feverishness, and he, too, took to his bedroll on the floor of the half-wrecked house of a friend in the suburb of Ushida.

   _____

6. These four did not realize it, but they were coming down with the strange, capricious disease which came later to be know as radiation sickness.

   _____

7. It was that the atomic bomb had deposited some sort of poison on Hiroshima which would give off deadly emanations for seven years; nobody could go there all that time.

   _____

8. His son said, "Father, we can do nothing except make our mind up to consecrate our lives for the country.

   _____

9. The crux of the matter is whether total war in its present form is justifiable, even when it serves a just purpose.

   _____

Hiroshima Vocabulary Worksheet Chapter Four Page 2

Part II: Determining the Meaning--Match the vocabulary words to their definitions.

____ 1. talismanic   A. unpredictable
____ 2. yen   B. sense of bodily discomfort, depression or unease
____ 3. decrepit   C. worn out; broken down from use
____ 4. buffeted   D. basic, central, or critical point
____ 5. malaise   E. make sacred
____ 6. capricious   F. forced; battered
____ 7. emanations   G. magical
____ 8. consecrate   H. something that comes forth from a source
____ 9. crux   I. Japanese money

Hiroshima Vocabulary Worksheet Chapter 5

Chapter Five Part I: Using Prior Knowledge and Contextual Clues

Below are the sentences in which the vocabulary words appear in the text. Read the sentence. Use any clues you can find in the sentence combined with your prior knowledge, and write what you think the underlined words mean on the lines provided.

1. At this precarious time she fell ill.

_____

2. For more than a decade after the bombings, the hibakusha lived in an economic limbo, apparently because the Japanese government did not want to find itself saddled with anything like moral responsibility for heinous acts of the victorious United States.

_____

3. Two years earlier, a Quaker professor of dendrology for the University of Washington,...driven, apparently, by deep urges for epilation and reconciliation, had come to Hiroshima.

_____

4. His family had money—and, indeed, over the years it turned out (as it did for a great many Japanese doctors) that most efficacious medicine for whatever ailed him would be cash or credit, the larger the dosage the better.

_____

5. This was ostensibly for patients, but he opened it to the townspeople as well....

_____

6. He could face Hiroshima now, because a gaudy phoenix had risen from the ruinous desert of 1945:...a city of strivers and sybarites, with seven hundred and fifty-three bookstores and two thousand three hundred and fifty-six bars.

_____

7. She perceived the latter as confused boys of nineteen and twenty who as draftees were involved in a war they did not consider theirs, and who felt a rudimentary responsibility—or, at the very least, guilt—as fathers.

_____

8. Ever since his trip to America, he had wanted a house like that of one of the Mount Sinai doctors, and now, to her chagrin, he designed and built, next to the wooden house Shigeyuki was living in, a three-story concrete home for himself alone.

_____

Hiroshima Vocabulary Worksheet Chapter Five Page 2

Part II: Determining the Meaning -- Match the vocabulary words to their definitions.

_____ 1. precarious   A. represented or appearing as such
_____ 2. heinous   B. basic; at the roots
_____ 3. attitudinizing   C. assuming a false attitude; posturing
_____ 4. efficacious   D. dangerously lacking security of stability
_____ 5. ostensibly   E. producing the desired effect
_____ 6. sybarites   F. horrible; abominable; reprehensible
_____ 7. rudimentary   G. feeling of embarrassment or humiliation caused by failure or disappointment
_____ 8. chagrin   H. people devoted to pleasure and luxury

ANSWER KEY - VOCABULARY
Hiroshima

Chapter One	Chapter Two	Chapter Three	Chapter Four	Chapter Five
1. D	1. B	1. F	1. G	1. D
2. G	2. D	2. G	2. I	2. F
3. A	3. G	3. E	3. C	3. C
4. I	4. C	4. B	4. F	4. E
5. B	5. A	5. D	5. B	5. A
6. E	6. H	6. A	6. A	6. H
7. H	7. E	7. C	7. H	7. B
8. C	8. F	8. H	8. E	8. G
9. F			9. D	

DAILY LESSONS

LESSON ONE

<u>Objectives</u>
1. To introduce the unit
2. To find out what impressions/knowledge students already have about Hiroshima
3. To give students factual background information about Hiroshima

NOTES:
    Prior to this lesson you need to make arrangements to have a guest speaker come to your class to discuss the events leading up to the dropping of the bomb on Hiroshima. Look for a member of your local historical society, a history professor, or any person who has knowledge about these events and ask that person to come give your students background information about the dropping of the bomb on Hiroshima.

    Also prior to this lesson, you should prepare a bulletin board titled HIROSHIMA with blank background paper and the title.

<u>Activity #1</u>
    Ask students what words, ideas or facts come to their minds when they hear the words "Hiroshima" or "atomic bomb." Write students' responses on the bulletin board using different colored markers.

Transition: Explain to students that the book you will be reading is about the after-effects of the dropping of the bomb on Hiroshima. In additional preparation for reading that book, you have invited _ (fill in the person's name) _ to come to speak with them today about the events that led up to the dropping of the bomb.

<u>Activity #2</u>
    Have your guest speaker make his/her presentation to the class. Be sure to allow time for questions following the presentation.

LESSON TWO

Objectives
1. To distribute books and other related materials
2. To preview the study questions for Part One
3. To familiarize students with the vocabulary for Part One
4. To read Part One

Activity #1

Distribute the materials students will use in this unit. Explain in detail how students are to use these materials.

<u>Study Guides</u> Students should read the study guide questions for each reading assignment prior to beginning the reading assignment to get a feeling for what events and ideas are important in the section they are about to read. After reading the section, students will (as a class or individually) answer the questions to review the important events and ideas from that section of the book. Students should keep the study guides as study materials for the unit test.

<u>Vocabulary</u> Prior to reading a reading assignment, students will do vocabulary work related to the section of the book they are about to read. Following the completion of the reading of the book, there will be a vocabulary review of all the words used in the vocabulary assignments. Students should keep their vocabulary work as study materials for the unit test.

<u>Reading Assignment Sheet</u> You need to fill in the reading assignment sheet to let students know by when their reading has to be completed. You can either write the assignment sheet up on a side blackboard or bulletin board and leave it there for students to see each day, or you can "ditto" copies for each student to have. In either case, you should advise students to become very familiar with the reading assignments so they know what is expected of them.

<u>Extra Activities Center</u> The Unit Resource portion of this unit contains suggestions for an extra library of related books and articles in your classroom as well as crossword and word search puzzles. Make an extra activities center in your room where you will keep these materials for students to use. (Bring the books and articles in from the library and keep several copies of the puzzles on hand.) Explain to students that these materials are available for students to use when they finish reading assignments or other class work early.

<u>Nonfiction Assignment Sheet</u> Explain to students that they each are to read at least one non-fiction piece from the in-class library at some time during the unit. Students will fill out a nonfiction assignment sheet after completing the reading to help you evaluate their reading experiences and to help the students think about and evaluate their own reading experiences.

<u>Books</u> Each school has its own rules and regulations regarding student use of school books. Advise students of the procedures that are normal for your school.

Activity #3

Preview the study questions and show students how to do the vocabulary work for Part One of *Hiroshima*.

Activity #2

Have students read Part One of *Hiroshima* out loud in class. You probably know the best way to get readers with your class; pick students at random, ask for volunteers, or use whatever method works best for your group. If you have not yet completed an oral reading evaluation for your students this marking period, this would be a good opportunity to do so. A form is included with this unit for your convenience. If students don't finish this assignment in class, they should do so to the next class period.

NONFICTION ASSIGNMENT SHEET - *Hiroshima*
(To be completed after reading the required nonfiction article)

Name _____ Date _____

Title of Nonfiction Read _____

Written By _____ Publication Date _____

I. Factual Summary: Write a short summary of the piece you read.

II. Vocabulary
    1. With which vocabulary words in the piece did you encounter some degree of difficulty?

    2. How did you resolve your lack of understanding with these words?

III. Interpretation: What was the main point the author wanted you to get from reading his work?

IV. Criticism
    1. With which points of the piece did you agree or find easy to accept? Why?

    2. With which points of the piece did you disagree or find difficult to believe? Why?

V. Personal Response: What do you think about this piece? <u>OR</u> How does this piece influence your ideas?

ORAL READING EVALUATION - *Hiroshima*

Name _____ Class____ Date _____

SKILL	EXCELLENT	GOOD	AVERAGE	FAIR	POOR
Fluency	5	4	3	2	1
Clarity	5	4	3	2	1
Audibility	5	4	3	2	1
Pronunciation	5	4	3	2	1
_____	5	4	3	2	1
_____	5	4	3	2	1

Total _____   Grade _____

Comments:

LESSON THREE

<u>Objectives</u>
1. To review the main events and ideas from Part One
2. To preview the study questions for Part Two
3. To familiarize students with the vocabulary in Part Two
4. To read Part Two

<u>Activity #1</u>
Give students a few minutes to formulate answers for the study guide questions for Part One, and then discuss the answers to the questions in detail. Write the answers on the board or overhead transparency so students can have the correct answers for study purposes. Note: It is a good practice in public speaking and leadership skills for individual students to take charge of leading the discussions of the study questions. Perhaps a different student could go to the front of the class and lead the discussion each day that the study questions are discussed during this unit. Of course, the teacher should guide the discussion when appropriate and be sure to fill in any gaps the students leave.

<u>Activity #2</u>
Give students about fifteen minutes to preview the study questions for Part Two of *Hiroshima* and to do the related vocabulary work.

<u>Activity #3</u>
Assign students to read Part Two of *Hiroshima* prior to your next class period. If time remains in this class period, continue the oral reading evaluations as students begin to read Part Two.

LESSON FOUR

Objectives
1. To check to see that students read Part Two as assigned
2. To review the main ideas and events from Part Two

Activity #1

Quiz - Distribute quizzes and give students about 10 minutes to complete them. (Note: The quizzes may either be the short answer study guides or the multiple choice version for Part Two.) Have students exchange papers. Grade the quizzes as a class. Collect the papers for recording the grades. (If you used the multiple choice version as a quiz, take a few minutes to discuss the answers for the short answer version if your students are using the short answer version for their study guides.)

Activity #2

Tell students (or copy this onto a transparency and read it with students):

The dropping of the bomb on Hiroshima was a whopper of an event affecting literally millions of people all over the world. Every day on the news we hear of robberies, murders, accidents, diseases, wars and other tragedies. Most of the time the news tells about things that happened to someone else -- not to us -- and we are at least somewhat insulated from the reality of the situations. Most of the time we listen to the news and think, "That's terrible" or "Gee, what a shame. I really feel sorry for those people." And the next night we're bombarded with a whole new set of characters in a whole new set of tragedies. It is rare that we get any follow up on any of the people who are involved.

Once and a while, we should stop to remember that for each news item reported, a certain number of people's lives change forever. We should not lose our feelings of sympathy or empathy for the many people involved; we should not allow ourselves to become too dulled and emotionally numb from the barrage of tragedies that we hear about each day. We must try to remain alert and empathetic and to try to find ways to not only help those who are hurt but also to reduce the number of senseless tragedies that happen in our world.

Your assignment is to find a newspaper account of a tragic event, read it, and fill out the Point of View Worksheet you are about to receive. After you have had time to complete this assignment, we will discuss your worksheets.

Distribute the worksheets and give students ample time to complete them. This unit plan calls for the discussion of the worksheets in Lesson Six.

POINT OF VIEW WORKSHEET - *Hiroshima*

Summary - Write a summary of the facts of your news article.

People - Make a list of the people who are involved in the event and their roles in the event.
Example: Mr. Smith - the victim - his store was robbed

Person/Name	Role

Hiroshima Point of View Worksheet Page 2

<u>Others</u> - Identify other people who could be affected by this event even though they were not at the scene.

<u>Effects</u> Explain how each person involved (either directly or indirectly) could be affected by this event.

Person	Effect of the Event

Hiroshima Point of View Worksheet Page 3

Other Effects - Could this event have other, further reaching effects? If so, what could they be?

Reactions - Identify how each of the people involved probably feels now that the event has happened.

What is *your* reaction to the event?

Hiroshima Point of View Worksheet Page 4

Coping - Now you know what happened and how the people involved probably feel, how do you think the people involved will cope with their situations?

Changes - Will the lives of any of the people involved change because of this event? If so, whose lives will change, and how will they change?

Prevention - Could the event have been prevented? What things might have helped to prevent the event?

LESSON FIVE

Objectives
1. To preview Part Three
2. To read Part Three
3. To continue the Point of View assignment from Lesson Four

Activity #1
Give students about fifteen minutes to preview the study questions for Part Three of *Hiroshima* and to do the related vocabulary work.

Activity #3
Assign students to read Part Three of *Hiroshima* prior to your next class period. Students may read Part Three silently in class. If students complete the reading assignment before the end of the class period, they should continue working on the Point of View assignments from Lesson Four.

LESSON SIX

Objectives
1. To review the main ideas and events from Part Three
2. To conclude the Point of View Assignments

Activity #1
Give students a few minutes to formulate answers to the study questions for Part Three and then discuss their answers in detail.

Activity #2
Have each student give a short, oral summary of the article he/she used for the Point of View assignment. Take a couple of minutes to discuss the impact and implications of each event that took place. The purpose of this activity is *not* to bombard students with more bad news; it is to help students learn to assess and empathize, and to show students ways people can cope with tragedy and go on with their lives.

LESSON SEVEN

Objectives
    1. To preview Part Four
    2. To read Part Four

Activity #1

    Give students about fifteen minutes to preview the study questions for Part Four of *Hiroshima* and to do the related vocabulary work.

Activity #3

    Assign students to read Part Four of *Hiroshima* prior to your next class period. Students may read Part Three silently in class.

LESSON EIGHT

Objectives
    1. To review the main ideas and events from Part Four
    2. To familiarize students with Japan's history, culture, and role in the world

Activity #1

    Give students a few minutes to formulate answers to the study questions for Part Four and then discuss their answers in detail.

Activity #2

    Take students to the library/media center. Distribute the Research Assignment Sheets. Discuss the directions in detail and give students time to work on the assignment.

RESEARCH ASSIGNMENT - *Hiroshima*

PROMPT

The dropping of The Bomb on Hiroshima was an emotional event for millions of people all around the world, and it was a politically important event which is still influencing politics and global relations today. Through reading John Hersey's book *Hiroshima* you have learned some things about Japan. But who *are* the Japanese people? What is their heritage, their culture, and their place in the world since the bombing of Hiroshima?

ASSIGNMENT

Your assignment is to create a video titled *Japan Today*. In this video, you will need to give some information about Japan's cultural heritage and history as background for understanding Japan today. The main thrust of your video, though, is to show how Japan is today. Each of you will prepare a five-minute segment which will be taped and put together into a finished video. The topic assignment chart below will show you your topic.

You should have visual materials the video camera will record as you narrate your segment. In other words, we're not going to just take a video of you reading a report. You should prepare some relevant visual materials that can be filmed as you read your report. They can be pictures, timeline(s), models, drawings, photographs, a segment of video tape with a skit -- anything relevant and visual.

GETTING STARTED

Use any resources you can find to get information about your topic: books, magazines, encyclopedias, movies, videos, travel brochures, interviews, etc. Begin here in the library. If you are using books, magazines or encyclopedias that also contain information others may need, read the article(s) and take notes so others will have the materials available for use later. Take notes and fill out a Nonfiction Reading Assignment Sheet for each nonfiction source you use.

SCHEDULE

You will have this class period to begin collecting information and materials. Then you will work on your own (out of class) for a few days. You will have one more class period to work in class on your presentation before the taping day. You will bring all of your materials to class (including Writing Assignment #1 - your script) on taping day.

Library <u>today</u>
In-class working session _____
Taping day _____

TOPIC ASSIGNMENTS - JAPAN

TOPIC	ASSIGNED TO
PHYSICAL FEATURES/MAP	
NATURAL RESOURCES	
ANCIENT HISTORY	
MODERN HISTORY	
CULTURE/TRADITIONS	
GOVERNMENT	
CLIMATE/VEGETATION/ANIMAL LIFE	
SOCIETY AND FAMILY	
CITIES	
RELIGION	
LANGUAGE	
ART	
LITERATURE	
SCIENCE/TECHNOLOGY	
EDUCATION	
HEALTH AND WELFARE	
ECONOMY	
MANUFACTURING	
TRANSPORTATION/COMMUNICATION	
INTERNATIONAL RELATIONS	
CURRENT EVENTS (LAST 5 YEARS)	
CURRENT EVENTS (LAST 5 YEARS)	
SPORTS	
TRADE RELATIONS	
JAPAN IN WORLD WAR II	

WRITING ASSIGNMENT #1 - *Hiroshima*

PROMPT

Before you create your five-minute video segment, you need to decide exactly what you will say, what visuals you will be using, and how the two are going to fit together. Your assignment is to write a script for your five minute video segment.

PREWRITING

Much of your prewriting has been done as you have taken notes and have done your research. You should have a pretty big pile of information from which you can select to create your five minute segment.

Your first step should be to select the information you wish to use. Remember you only have five minutes, so you must choose your information carefully. You don't have enough time to get involved with a lot of details. What you need to do is to give an overview of your topic; tell us what we most need to know about your topic. Likewise, don't get stuck on only one facet of your topic. Cover a wide range of information and give the most important main ideas.

Take your notes and circle the points you think should be included in your video segment. (If you have taken notes on index cards, pull out the cards you think have the most important information.)

Next, organize your information. Put it in a logical order that will be easily understood by your audience. The easiest way to do this is to make a little outline. You may need to revise your outline several times as you think about your material and your presentation.

Look at what you have. Do a brief calculation as to how much time it will take you to cover the material you have selected. If you need more, go back to your notes and add things. If you think you have too much material to cover in five minutes, go through your outline and delete some of the information.

After you have chosen the content for your segment, think about what visuals you will use. To the left of your outline, make a few notes as to what people will be seeing as you narrate. Now that you have considered your visuals, you may wish to rearrange your presentation and re-do your outline to make the most effective presentation possible.

DRAFTING

Follow your outline and write out exactly what you will say to narrate your five minute segment about your topic. Make a real effort to vary your sentence structure so you don't fall into the short sentence (fact) followed by short sentence (fact) followed by short sentence (fact) etc. rut. Make your presentation as interesting as possible. (Pretend you were watching the finished Japan video in class -- what would make it interesting for you?)

PROMPT

When you finish the rough draft of your paper, ask a student who sits near you to read it. After reading your rough draft, he/she should tell you what he/she liked best about your work, which parts were difficult to understand, and ways in which your work could be improved. Reread your paper considering your critic's comments, and make the necessary corrections.

LESSON NINE

Objectives
1. To preview the study questions and vocabulary for Part Five
2. To read Part Five

Activity #1
Give students ample time to preview the study questions and to do the prereading vocabulary worksheet for Part Five.

Activity #2
If you have not yet completed the oral reading evaluations, have students read Part Five orally in class and complete the evaluations. If you have completed the evaluations, students may read silently during the remainder of this class period.

LESSON TEN

Objectives
1. To review the main ideas and events from Part Five
2. To discuss the book on interpretive and critical levels

Activity #1
Give students a few minutes to formulate answers for the study questions for Part Five of *Hiroshima*. Discuss the answers in detail. Jot down the correct answers on the board or overhead for students to copy down for study use later.

Activity #2
Choose the questions from the Extra Discussion Questions/Writing Assignments which seem most appropriate for your students. A class discussion of these questions is most effective if students have been given the opportunity to formulate answers to the questions prior to the discussion. To this end, you may either have all the students formulate answers to all the questions, divide your class into groups and assign one or more questions to each group, or you could assign one question to each student in your class. The option you choose will make a difference in the amount of class time needed for this activity.

Activity #3
After students have had ample time to formulate answers to the questions, begin your class discussion of the questions and the ideas presented by the questions. Be sure students take notes during the discussion so they have information to study for the unit test.

EXTRA DISCUSSION QUESTIONS & WRITING ASSIGNMENTS - *Hiroshima*

Interpretive

1. From what point of view is *Hiroshima* written, and what effect does that have on the story?

2. Is there a climax in *Hiroshima*? If so, where is it? If not, why isn't there one?

3. Make a list of the technical details given in the story and discuss their effect on the story.

4. Write a character sketch of each of the six survivors.

Critical/Personal Response

5. Why did John Hersey chose to write about these six particular people? What did he (and we) gain by seeing the bombing and its effects through the eyes of *these* six people?

6. Characterize John Hersey's style of writing. How does it contribute to the value of the book?

7. In what ways is *Hiroshima* different from other stories?

8. Choose another title for the book and explain your choice.

Personal Response

9. Why did the United States drop the bombs on Hiroshima and Nagasaki?

10. Did you enjoy reading *Hiroshima*? Why or why not?

11. Was the use of the bomb justifiable at the time it was dropped?

12. Is there or could/should there be a limit to actions which can be taken in a war?

13. If the Japanese had developed the atomic bomb first, do you think they would have used it against the United States?

14. What should we learn from the bombing of Hiroshima?

15. Summarize Japanese-American relations from 1945 to the present.

16. Summarize Japan's involvement in World War II.

LESSON ELEVEN

Objective
To review all of the vocabulary work done in this unit

Activity
Choose one (or more) of the vocabulary review activities listed below and spend your class period as directed in the activity. Some of the materials for these review activities are located in the Unit Resource section in this unit.

VOCABULARY REVIEW ACTIVITIES

1. Divide your class into two teams and have an old-fashioned spelling or definition bee.

2. Give each of your students (or students in groups of two, three or four) a *Hiroshima* Vocabulary Word Search Puzzle. The person (group) to find all of the vocabulary words in the puzzle first wins.

3. Give students a *Hiroshima* Vocabulary Word Search Puzzle without the word list. The person or group to find the most vocabulary words in the puzzle wins.

4. Use a *Hiroshima* Vocabulary Crossword Puzzle. Put the puzzle onto a transparency on the overhead projector (so everyone can see it), and do the puzzle together as a class.

5. Give students a *Hiroshima* Vocabulary Matching Worksheet to do.

6. Divide your class into two teams. Use the *Hiroshima* vocabulary words with their letters jumbled as a word list. Student 1 from Team A faces off against Student 1 from Team B. You write the first jumbled word on the board. The first student (1A or 1B) to unscramble the word wins the chance for his/her team to score points. If 1A wins the jumble, go to student 2A and give him/her a definition. He/she must give you the correct spelling of the vocabulary word which fits that definition. If he/she does, Team A scores a point, and you give student 3A a definition for which you expect a correctly spelled matching vocabulary word. Continue giving Team A definitions until some team member makes an incorrect response. An incorrect response sends the game back to the jumbled-word face off, this time with students 2A and 2B. Instead of repeating giving definitions to the first few students of each team, continue with the student after the one who gave the last incorrect response on the team. For example, if Team B wins the jumbled-word face-off, and student 5B gave the last incorrect answer for Team B, you would start this round of definition questions with student 6B, and so on. The team with the most points wins!

7. Have students write a story in which they correctly use as many vocabulary words as possible. Have students read their compositions orally! Post the most original compositions on your bulletin board!

LESSON TWELVE

Objective
To give students the opportunity to work on their research/video assignments

Activity
Give students this class period to work on their Japan research assignments. Since the narration should be written already, students should use this class period to work on their visuals. If some students have completed both their narrations and visuals, be prepared to begin filming their segments.

LESSON THIRTEEN

Objectives
1. To further discuss the ideas presented in the book
2. To give students a chance to work together in small groups to exchange ideas and find information
3. To develop a composite time-line showing the main activities of all six survivors

Activity #1
Divide your class into 6 groups - one group for each survivor Hersey follows in the book. The group members should get together and make a timeline showing the main activities of their group's character.

Activity #3
Call on the groups to report the information they were able to compile. Make one huge timeline on the board (or overhead projector transparency) showing all of the characters' main activities in relationship to each other with time as a constant.

LESSON FOURTEEN

<u>Objectives</u>
1. To give students the opportunity to practice writing to persuade
2. To make students think about the event of the dropping of the bomb on Hiroshima and to determine their own feelings about it
3. To give the teacher the opportunity to evaluate students' writing skills

<u>Activity</u>
    Distribute Writing Assignment #2. Discuss the directions in detail and give students ample time to complete the assignment.

LESSONS FIFTEEN AND SIXTEEN

<u>Objectives</u>
1. To compile the Japan research projects
2. To film students' five-minute segments
3. To help students study their vocabulary words

<u>Activities</u>
    If you have not already done so, begin filming students' five-minute segments about Japan. Students who have not yet been filmed may silently review their own narrations while you film other students. Students who have been filmed may watch the segment(s) being filmed or could do vocabulary or unit review worksheets/puzzles while you are working with other students.

LESSON SEVENTEEN

<u>Objectives</u>
1. To give students a wide variety of information about Japan
2. To conclude the research assignments
3. To show students the finished product that they have created

<u>Activity</u>
    Show the class the complete film of their individual five-minute segments about Japan.

WRITING ASSIGNMENT #2 - *Hiroshima*

PROMPT

People usually have strong feelings one way or the other about the dropping of the bombs on Japan. Some people think that the United States was completely justified in dropping the bombs because it saved thousands of American lives, it ended the war more quickly than any other means, and because "all is fair in love and war." Other people believe that the dropping of the bombs was an outrage, too cruel, inhuman -- that the United States stepped over the boundary line of what is acceptable in civilized warfare.

Your assignment is to consider the two sides of the issue, decide which side you believe in, and write an essay in which you convince someone who believes the opposite that your side is right.

PREWRITING

Much of your background work has been done through your reading, research, and class discussions. Decide which side of this issue you believe. As you are making your decision, write down the ideas that influence your decision. What things are most important? Go back and look at these ideas. Write down the three best arguments for the case that the United Stated should (or shouldn't) have done what it did.

DRAFTING

Write a paragraph in which you introduce the idea that the dropping of the bombs on Japan was (or wasn't) what the United States should have done.

In the body of your composition, write one paragraph for each of the three arguments you decided upon in the prewriting stage above. Use a topic sentence for each paragraph (stating the argument) and fill in each paragraph with examples, facts and/or ideas that support your argument.

Write a paragraph in which you conclude your arguments and close your composition.

PROMPT

When you finish the rough draft of your paper, ask a student who sits near you to read it. After reading your rough draft, he/she should tell you what he/she liked best about your work, which parts were difficult to understand, and ways in which your work could be improved. Reread your paper considering your critic's comments, and make the corrections you think are necessary.

PROOFREADING

Do a final proofreading of your paper double-checking your grammar, spelling, organization, and the clarity of your ideas.

LESSON EIGHTEEN

Objectives
    1. To give students the opportunity to practice writing their own personal opinions
    2. To give the teacher the opportunity to evaluate students' writing skills
    3. To have students think about the role of Japan in the world in the near future
    4. To have students rewrite assignment 1 and/or 2

Activity #1
    Distribute Writing Assignment #3. Discuss the directions in detail and give students ample time to complete the assignment.

Activity #2
    While students are working on Writing Assignment #3, call individual students to your desk or some other private area for a writing conference using Writing Assignment #1 and Writing Assignment #2 as the basis for your conferences. An evaluation form is included with this unit to help you structure your conferences, should you choose to use it. Have students rewrite/revise their first writing assignment(s) taking your suggestions into consideration. Be sure to tell students when their revisions should be completed.

LESSON NINETEEN

Objectives
    To review the main ideas presented in *Hiroshima*

Activity #1
    Choose one of the review games/activities included in this unit and spend your class period as outlined there. Some materials for these activities are located in the Extra Activities section of this unit.

Activity #2
    Remind students that the Unit Test will be in the next class meeting. Stress the review of the Study Guides and their class notes as a last minute, brush-up review for homework.

WRITING ASSIGNMENT #3 - *Hiroshima*

PROMPT

Japan has become a major player in world economics, manufacturing everything from cars to computers, televisions to tape players (and much more). You have learned many things about Japan. Use that knowledge combined with your knowledge of the world to write a composition in which you give your opinions about what Japan's role in the world will be for the next fifty years.

PREWRITING

Most of your prewriting has been done through class discussions and your own research. Organize your own thoughts now and decide how (if at all) you think Japan will be influencing world events over the next fifty years. Jot down your ideas as you think of them -- and any reasons why you believe these ideas to be true. After you are done brainstorming ideas, go back and organize them.

DRAFTING

Write a paragraph in which you introduce your ideas of what you think Japan's role will be in the future.

In the body of your composition, write one paragraph for each of your main points, using topic sentences and examples, facts or other statements which support your idea(s) to fill out the paragraphs.

Write a paragraph in which you make your final conclusions and bring your composition to a close.

PROMPT

When you finish the rough draft of your paper, ask a student who sits near you to read it. After reading your rough draft, he/she should tell you what he/she liked best about your work, which parts were difficult to understand, and ways in which your work could be improved. Reread your paper considering your critic's comments, and make the corrections you think are necessary.

PROOFREADING

Do a final proofreading of your paper double-checking your grammar, spelling, organization, and the clarity of your ideas.

WRITING EVALUATION FORM - *Hiroshima*

Name _____ Date _____

    Grade _____

Circle One For Each Item:

Grammar:		excellent		good	fair	poor

Spelling:		excellent		good	fair	poor

Punctuation:		excellent		good	fair	poor

Legibility:		excellent		good	fair	poor

Strengths:

Weaknesses:

Comments/Suggestions:

REVIEW GAMES/ACTIVITIES - *Hiroshima*

1. Ask the class to make up a unit test for *Hiroshima*. The test should have 4 sections: matching, true/false, short answer, and essay. Students may use 1/2 period to make the test and then swap papers and use the other 1/2 class period to take a test a classmate has devised. (open book) You may want to use the unit test included in this unit or take questions from the students' unit tests to formulate your own test.

2. Take 1/2 period for students to make up true and false questions (including the answers). Collect the papers and divide the class into two teams. Draw a big tic-tac-toe board on the chalk board. Make one team X and one team O. Ask questions to each side, giving each student one turn. If the question is answered correctly, that students' team's letter (X or O) is placed in the box. If the answer is incorrect, no mark is placed in the box. The object is to get three marks in a row like tic-tac-toe. You may want to keep track of the number of games won for each team.

3. Take 1/2 period for students to make up questions (true/false and short answer). Collect the questions. Divide the class into two teams. You'll alternate asking questions to individual members of teams A & B (like in a spelling bee). The question keeps going from A to B until it is correctly answered, then a new question is asked. A correct answer does not allow the team to get another question. Correct answers are +2 points; incorrect answers are -1 point.

4. Have students pair up and quiz each other from their study guides and class notes.

5. Give students a *Hiroshima* crossword puzzle to complete.

6. Divide your class into two teams. Use the *Hiroshima* crossword words with their letters jumbled as a word list. Student 1 from Team A faces off against Student 1 from Team B. You write the first jumbled word on the board. The first student (1A or 1B) to unscramble the word wins the chance for his/her team to score points. If 1A wins the jumble, go to student 2A and give him/her a clue. He/she must give you the correct word which matches that clue. If he/she does, Team A scores a point, and you give student 3A a clue for which you expect another correct response. Continue giving Team A clues until some team member makes an incorrect response. An incorrect response sends the game back to the jumbled-word face off, this time with students 2A and 2B. Instead of repeating giving clues to the first few students of each team, continue with the student after the one who gave the last incorrect response on the team. For example, if Team B wins the jumbled-word face-off, and student 5B gave the last incorrect answer for Team B, you would start this round of clue questions with student 6B, and so on. The team with the most points wins!

UNIT TESTS

SHORT ANSWER UNIT TEST 1 - *Hiroshima*

I. Matching/Identify

____ 1. Asano   A. City on which the second bomb was dropped

____ 2. Fujii   B. Author

____ 3. Hersey   C. Clerk at East Asia Tin Works trapped under bookcases

____ 4. Kleinsorge   D. ____ Park

____ 5. Kyo   E. Tailor's widow with small children

____ 6. Nagasaki   F. Pastor of Hiroshima Methodist Church

____ 7. Nakamura   G. Doctor who owned and operated a private hospital

____ 8. Sasaki   H. River near the park

____ 9. Saski   I. German priest

____ 10. Tanimoto   J. Doctor at Red Cross hospital; became wealthy

II. Short Answer

1. On what date, at what time, and where was the first atomic bomb set off?

2. Why did the atomic bomb take the Japanese by surprise? Why were they not expecting it?

3. At first there were very few fires. Why were so many people burned?

4. What were the estimated casualties just after the bomb hit?

Hiroshima Short Answer Unit Test 1 Page 2

5. Why did the people go to the park and to the river?

6. What were the survivors called? What did the name mean? Why was it chosen?

7. What were the three stages of radiation sickness?

8. What was unusual about the way the bomb affected the people at the time of its explosion?

9. The doctor at the East Parade Ground said his first duty was to take care of the slightly wounded. Why?

10. What happened at two minutes after eleven o'clock on the morning of August 9th?

III. Essay

    What was the point of the book *Hiroshima*? Why did the author bother to write it? Use examples from the text to support your statements when appropriate.

Hiroshima Short Answer Unit Test 1 Page 4

IV. Vocabulary

Listen to the vocabulary words and write them down. Go back later and write down the correct definition for each word.

1.

2.

3.

4.

5.

6.

7.

8.

9.

10.

KEY: SHORT ANSWER UNIT TEST #1 - *Hiroshima*

I. Matching/Identify

__D_ 1. Asano   A. City on which the second bomb was dropped

__G_ 2. Fujii   B. Author

__B_ 3. Hersey   C. Clerk at East Asia Tin Works trapped under bookcases

__I_ 4. Kleinsorge   D. ____ Park

__H_ 5. Kyo   E. Tailor's widow with small children

__A_ 6. Nagasaki   F. Pastor of Hiroshima Methodist Church

__E_ 7. Nakamura   G. Doctor who owned and operated a private hospital

__J_ 8. Sasaki   H. River near the park

__C_ 9. Saski   I. German priest

__F_ 10. Tanimoto   J. Doctor at Red Cross hospital; became wealthy

II. Short Answer

1. On what date, at what time, and where was the first atomic bomb set off?
    It was set off at fifteen minutes past eight in the morning on August 6, 1945 over the city of Hiroshima, Japan.

2. Why did the atomic bomb take the Japanese by surprise? Why were they not expecting it?
    The warning siren went off at seven and the people went to their "safe areas." At eight o'clock, the all clear siren sounded. Because the atomic bomb was dropped by a single plane, the plane was not seen as a threat, and no warning siren was given. So at 8:15 when the bomb was dropped, the citizens of Hiroshima were totally off-guard.

3. At first there were very few fires. Why were so many people burned?
    The people suffered radiation burns.

4. What were the estimated casualties just after the bomb hit?
    "In a city of 245,000, nearly a hundred thousand people had been killed or doomed at one blow; a hundred thousand more were hurt."

5. Why did the people go to the park and to the river?

    The park was designated as a safe area, it had not been destroyed by the bomb, and they thought that if the Americans would return, they would only bomb buildings. They went to the river to escape the fires which the winds were blowing out of control, and the people were thirsty and drank from the river.

6. What were the survivors called? What did the name mean? Why was it chosen?

    ". . . The Japanese tended to shy away from the term 'survivors,' because in its focus on being alive, it might suggest some slight to the sacred dead. The class of people to which the Nakamura-san belonged came, therefore, to be called by a more neutral name, 'hibakusha' – literally, 'explosion-affected persons.'"

7. What were the three stages of radiation sickness?

    Stage one occurred at the moment when the bomb went off. Apparently uninjured people died due to overdoses of radiation. "The rays simply destroyed body cells -- caused their nuclei to degenerate and broke their walls." The second stage set in ten or fifteen days after the bombing. Its symptoms were falling hair, diarrhea, and fever. Also blood disorders appeared in the second stage. White blood cell counts dropped, and small hemorrhages appeared on the skin and mucous membranes. Patients also suffered anemia. In the third stage, the body struggled to compensate for its ills. For instance, the white count not only returned to normal, but increased to much higher than normal levels. Complications also occurred in this stage.

8. What was unusual about the way the bomb affected the people at the time of its explosion?

    The people saw a bright light and then were suddenly picked up and moved by a great, unseen force. There was no noise of explosion following the bomb. There was a huge dust cloud which the people thought was just in their local areas and which made the day grow dark.

9. The doctor at the East Parade Ground said his first duty was to take care of the slightly wounded. Why?

    "In an emergency like this, the first task is to help as many as possible -- to save as many lives as possible. There is no hope for the heavily wounded. They will die. We can't bother with them."

10. What happened at two minutes after eleven o'clock on the morning of August 9th?

    The second atomic bomb was dropped on Nagasaki.

III. Essay: Answers will vary.

IV. Vocabulary: Choose ten of the vocabulary words. Read them orally to your class so the students can write them down on part IV of their vocabulary tests.

SHORT ANSWER UNIT TEST 2 - *Hiroshima*

I. Matching

____ 1. Asano   A. Clerk at East Asia Tin Works trapped under bookcases

____ 2. Fujii   B. Doctor who owned and operated a private hospital

____ 3. Hersey   C. City on which the second bomb was dropped

____ 4. Kleinsorge   D. Author

____ 5. Kyo   E. German priest

____ 6. Nagasaki   F. Doctor at Red Cross hospital; became wealthy

____ 7. Nakamura   G. ____ Park

____ 8. Sasaki   H. Tailor's widow with small children

____ 9. Saski   I. River near the park

____ 10. Tanimoto   J. Pastor of Hiroshima Methodist Church

II. Short Answer

1. On what date, at what time, and where was the first atomic bomb set off?

2. Why did the atomic bomb take the Japanese by surprise? Why were they not expecting it?

3. What was unusual about the way the bomb affected the people at the time of its explosion?

4. Mr. Tanimoto, like the other survivors, was amazed when he looked out over the city after the bomb. Why?

Hiroshima Short Answer Unit Test 2 Page 2

5. What were the estimated casualties just after the bomb hit?

6. Why did the people go to the park and to the river?

7. Why did many people die in the river?

8. The doctor at the East Parade Ground said his first duty was to take care of the slightly wounded. Why?

9. A few weeks to a month after the bomb, what symptoms were people having?

10. On September 17th, another disaster happened at Hiroshima. What was it?

11. What were the three stages of radiation sickness?

12. What were the survivors called? What did the name mean? Why was it chosen?

Hiroshima Short Answer Unit Test 2 Page 3

III. Composition

    The <u>Saturday Review of Literature</u> said about the book *Hiroshima*, "Everyone able to read should read it." Using your knowledge of the book and information you've learned in class, defend that statement. Why should everyone read it?

IV. Vocabulary - Listen to the words and write them down. Go back later and write in the correct definition for each word.

1.

2.

3.

4.

5.

6.

7.

8.

9.

10.

KEY: SHORT ANSWER UNIT TEST 2 *Hiroshima*

I. Matching (Use this matching key also for the Advanced Short Answer Unit Test)

_G_ 1. Asano	A.	Clerk at East Asia Tin Works trapped under bookcases
_B_ 2. Fujii	B.	Doctor who owned and operated a private hospital
_D_ 3. Hersey	C.	City on which the second bomb was dropped
_E_ 4. Kleinsorge	D.	Author
_I_ 5. Kyo	E.	German priest
_C_ 6. Nagasaki	F.	Doctor at Red Cross hospital; became wealthy
_H_ 7. Nakamura	G.	____ Park
_F_ 8. Sasaki	H.	Tailor's widow with small children
_A_ 9. Saski	I.	River near the park
_J_ 10. Tanimoto	J.	Pastor of Hiroshima Methodist Church

II. Short Answer

1. On what date, at what time, and where was the first atomic bomb set off?
    It was set off at fifteen minutes past eight in the morning on August 6, 1945 over the city of Hiroshima, Japan.

2. Why did the atomic bomb take the Japanese by surprise? Why were they not expecting it?
    The warning siren went off at seven and the people went to their "safe areas." At eight o'clock, the all clear siren sounded. Because the atomic bomb was dropped by a single plane, the plane was not seen as a threat, and no warning siren was given. So at 8:15 when the bomb was dropped, the citizens of Hiroshima were totally off-guard.

3. What was unusual about the way the bomb affected the people at the time of its explosion?
    The people saw a bright light and then were suddenly picked up and moved by a great, unseen force. There was no noise of explosion following the bomb. There was a huge dust cloud which the people thought was just in their local areas and which made the day grow dark.

4. Mr. Tanimoto, like the other survivors, was amazed when he looked out over the city after the bomb. Why?

> "Not just a patch of Koi, as he had expected, but as much of Hiroshima as he could see through the clouded air was giving off a thick, dreadful miasma. . . . He wondered how such extensive damage could have been dealt out of a silent sky."

5. What were the estimated casualties just after the bomb hit?

> "In a city of 245,000, nearly a hundred thousand people had been killed or doomed at one blow; a hundred thousand more were hurt."

6. Why did the people go to the park and to the river?

> The park was designated as a safe area, it had not been destroyed by the bomb, and they thought that if the Americans would return, they would only bomb buildings. They went to the river to escape the fires which the winds were blowing out of control, and the people were thirsty and drank from the river.

7. Why did many people die in the river?

> Frightened people in the park pushed closer to the river to escape the raging fires, and the people who were on the banks of the river were pushed in by the mob.

8. The doctor at the East Parade Ground said his first duty was to take care of the slightly wounded. Why?

> "In an emergency like this, the first task is to help as many as possible -- to save as many lives as possible. There is no hope for the heavily wounded. They will die. We can't bother with them."

9. A few weeks to a month after the bomb, what symptoms were people having?

> Some people had a feeling of extreme weakness, of being tired. Others were beginning to have spot hemorrhages. Many people were losing their hair.

10. On September 17th, another disaster happened at Hiroshima. What was it?

> There was a cloud burst and then a typhoon. The flood took up where the bomb left off and caused more destruction.

11. What were the three stages of radiation sickness?

> Stage one occurred at the moment when the bomb went off. Apparently uninjured people died due to overdoses of radiation. "The rays simply destroyed body cells -- caused their nuclei to degenerate and broke their walls." The second stage set in ten or fifteen days after the bombing. Its symptoms were falling hair, diarrhea, and fever. Also blood disorders appeared in the second stage. White blood cell counts dropped, and small hemorrhages appeared on the skin and mucous membranes. Patients also suffered anemia. In the third stage, the body

struggled to compensate for its ills. For instance, the white count not only returned to normal, but increased to much higher than normal levels. Complications also occurred in this stage.

12. What were the survivors called? What did the name mean? Why was it chosen?
". . . The Japanese tended to shy away from the term 'survivors,' because in its focus on being alive, it might suggest some slight to the sacred dead. The class of people to which the Nakamura-san belonged came, therefore, to be called by a more neutral name, 'hibakusha' – literally, 'explosion-affected persons.'"

III. Composition: answers will vary.

IV. Vocabulary
Choose ten vocabulary words and read them orally to your class so students can write them down.

ADVANCED SHORT ANSWER UNIT TEST - *Hiroshima*

I. Matching

____ 1. Asano   A. Clerk at East Asia Tin Works trapped under bookcases

____ 2. Fujii   B. Doctor who owned and operated a private hospital

____ 3. Hersey   C. City on which the second bomb was dropped

____ 4. Kleinsorge   D. Author

____ 5. Kyo   E. German priest

____ 6. Nagasaki   F. Doctor at Red Cross hospital; became wealthy

____ 7. Nakamura   G. ____ Park

____ 8. Sasaki   H. Tailor's widow with small children

____ 9. Saski   I. River near the park

____ 10. Tanimoto   J. Pastor of Hiroshima Methodist Church

II. Composition - Answer each of the following with at least a complete paragraph.

1. On what date and why did the United States drop the bomb on Hiroshima?

Hiroshima Advanced Short Answer Unit Test Page 2

2. What is radiation sickness? How does one get it, and what are the symptoms of each of its stages?

3. What were the physical and political effects of the dropping of the bomb on Hiroshima?

4. Describe the current relationship between Japan and the United States.

Hiroshima Advanced Short Answer Unit Test Page 3

5. Choose one adjective to describe the book *Hiroshima* and defend your choice of words using examples from the book.

6. <u>The New York Times</u> said, "Nothing can be said about this book that can equal what the book has to say. It speaks for itself, and in an unforgettable way, for humanity." What does the book *Hiroshima* say?

Hiroshima Advanced Short Answer Unit Test Page 4

III. Vocabulary

    Write down the vocabulary words you are given. Go back later and use all of those vocabulary words in a composition relating to *Hiroshima*.

MULTIPLE CHOICE UNIT TEST 1 - *Hiroshima*

I. Matching/Identify

____ 1. Asano   A. City on which the second bomb was dropped

____ 2. Fujii   B. Author

____ 3. Hersey   C. Clerk at East Asia Tin Works trapped under bookcases

____ 4. Kleinsorge   D. ____ Park

____ 5. Kyo   E. Tailor's widow with small children

____ 6. Nagasaki   F. Pastor of Hiroshima Methodist Church

____ 7. Nakamura   G. Doctor who owned and operated a private hospital

____ 8. Sasaki   H. River near the park

____ 9. Saski   I. German priest

____ 10. Tanimoto   J. Doctor at Red Cross hospital; became wealthy

II. Multiple Choice

1. On what date, and at what time, and where was the first atomic bomb set off?
   - A. It was set off at half past nine in the evening on July 4, 1944, over the city of Hiroshima, Korea.
   - B. It was set off at fifteen minutes past eight in the morning on August 6, 1945, over the city of Hiroshima, Japan.
   - C. It was set off at noon on August 23, 1945, over the city of Hiroshima, Viet Nam.
   - D. It was set of at noon on August 23, 1945, over the city of Hiroshima, Formosa.

2. Why did the atomic bomb take the inhabitants by surprise?
   - A. They had been told the war was over.
   - B. No one believed the United States had the scientific capability of building such a bomb.
   - C. There had been so many recent scares and warning sirens that the people were starting to ignore them.
   - D. Only one plane was seen in the sky, and it was not thought of as dangerous.

Hiroshima Multiple Choice Unit Test 1 Page 2

3. The survivors were amazed when they looked out over the city after the bomb. Why?
    A. The entire city was on fire.
    B. There were no buildings standing.
    C. Much of the city was giving off a thick, dreadful miasma.
    D. The city was in much better shape physically than anyone had expected it to be.

4. Why were so many people burned?
    A. They were burned in the severe fires that started immediately after the explosion.
    B. Many people stayed outside to look at the damage, and were sunburned.
    C. They suffered radiation burns.
    D. Many people were cooking over open fires when the bomb was dropped, and had kitchen fires.

5. What were the estimated casualties just after the bomb hit?
    A. Nearly 100,000 had been killed or doomed; 100,000 more were hurt.
    B. Half of the population, or 122,000 were either dead or wounded. The others were safe.
    C. All but 50 people in the city were dead.
    D. 200,000 were hurt, and 50,000 were dead.

6. Where did the people go to be safe?
    A. They went into the underground shelters.
    B. They went to the hospital, which was still standing.
    C. They went to the mountains.
    D. They went to the park and to the river.

7. Why were the people nauseated?
    A. They had radiation sickness, and had been drinking brackish water.
    B. They were sick from the gas the Americans had dropped.
    C. They were hungry and ill from exposure to the elements.
    D. It was fear combined with exhaustion.

8. One of the survivors was rescuing wounded people. What did he have to keep reminding himself while he did so?
    A. He tried to take the children and the elderly first.
    B. He wanted to help all of the people, regardless of the clan they belonged to.
    C. He was helping human beings.
    D. They were probably contagious, and he should try to keep his nose and mouth covered.

Hiroshima Multiple Choice Unit Test 1 Page 3

9. Who was the doctor at the East Parade Ground taking care of first?
    A. He was taking care of children and pregnant women, because they had no one else to look after them.
    B. He was taking care of the most seriously injured, to get them to perimeter hospitals and clear the area.
    C. He was taking care of the military personnel, so they could get back to work.
    D. He was taking care of the slightly wounded, in order to save as many lives as possible.

10. What happened at two minutes after eleven o'clock on the morning of August 9th?
    A. Japan retaliated and bombed Pearl Harbor.
    B. The war was officially ended and peace was declared.
    C. The was a huge earthquake that leveled the city and killed most of the bomb survivors.
    D. A second atomic bomb was dropped on Nagasaki.

11. When Miss Sasaki saw the ruins of Hiroshima for the first time, what gave her the creeps?
    A. There was a blanket of fresh, lush green, and wild flowers were blooming.
    B. There were skeletons all over the streets, and they were giving off a yellow-green glow.
    C. The city was deathly quiet.
    D. Everything was dark. There was no electricity, and the sun was hidden by a covering of smoke and ash.

12. A few weeks to a month after the bomb people were having many symptoms. Which of the following is not one of the symptoms?
    A. Feelings of extreme weakness.
    B. A wracking cough.
    C. Loss of hair.
    D. Spot hemorrhages.

13. On September 17th, another disaster happened at Hiroshima. What was it?
    A. There was an epidemic of smallpox.
    B. There was a 7.2 magnitude earthquake.
    C. The people were so scared and frustrated that they began rioting in the streets. Many were killed and injured, and the rioting lasted far into the night.
    D. There was a cloudburst and a typhoon, which caused a flood.

Hiroshima Multiple Choice Unit Test 1 Page 4

14. What disease was becoming common among the survivors?
    A. It was tuberculosis.
    B. It was leukemia.
    C. It was meningitis.
    D. It was hyperthyroidism.

15 Why did the survivors suffer for more than a decade after the bombings?
    A. The entire country was so depressed that no one could figure out what to do.
    B. The government did not want to find itself saddled with anything like moral responsibility for the heinous acts of the victorious United States.
    C. Most of the doctors and nurses had died, and there was no one to work on finding a cure.
    D. The people were trying to show the rest of the world that they regretted the Japanese involvement in the war. They saw their suffering as a means of atonement for the sins of their leaders.

III. Composition
Describe the physical and political effects of the dropping of the bomb on Hiroshima.

Hiroshima Multiple Choice Unit Test 1 Page 5

IV. Vocabulary - Match the correct definitions to the words.

____ 1. MALAISE	A. People devoted to pleasure and luxury

____ 2. HEDONISTIC	B. District administered or governed by a prefect

____ 3. BUFFETED	C. Represented or appearing as such

____ 4. PAROXYSM	D. Sense of bodily discomfort, depression or unease

____ 5. PUTRESCENCE	E. Basic, central or critical point

____ 6. EMANATIONS	F. Forced; battered

____ 7. PREFECTURAL	G. Sudden outburst

____ 8. EXTRICATED	H. Assuming a false attitude; posturing

____ 9. OSTENSIBLY	I. Pulled out

____ 10. SOLICITOUS	J. Exploration of an area to gather information

____ 11. TALISMANIC	K. Poisonous atmosphere

____ 12. ATAVISTIC	L. Characterized by the pursuit of sensual pleasure

____ 13. RECONNAISSANCE	M. Worn out; broken down from use

____ 14. APATHETIC	N. Magical

____ 15. ATTITUDINIZING	O. Uncaring; uninterested

____ 16. CRUX	P. Decomposed, rotten, foul-smelling matter

____ 17. MIASMA	Q. Scorched

____ 18. DECREPIT	R. Something that comes forth from a source

____ 19. CHARRED	S. Marked by anxious care and attentiveness

____ 20. SYBARITES	T. Return of a trait after a period of absence

MULTIPLE CHOICE UNIT TEST 2 - *Hiroshima*

I. Matching

___ 1. Asano   A. Clerk at East Asia Tin Works trapped under bookcases

___ 2. Fujii   B. Doctor who owned and operated a private hospital

___ 3. Hersey   C. City on which the second bomb was dropped

___ 4. Kleinsorge   D. Author

___ 5. Kyo   E. German priest

___ 6. Nagasaki   F. Doctor at Red Cross hospital; became wealthy

___ 7. Nakamura   G. ____ Park

___ 8. Sasaki   H. Tailor's widow with small children

___ 9. Saski   I. River near the park

___ 10. Tanimoto   J. Pastor of Hiroshima Methodist Church

II. Multiple Choice

1. On what date, and at what time, and where was the first atomic bomb set off?
    A. It was set off at fifteen minutes past eight in the morning on August 6, 1945, over the city of Hiroshima, Japan.
    B. It was set off at half past nine in the evening on July 4, 1944, over the city of Hiroshima, Korea.
    C. It was set off at noon on August 23, 1945, over the city of Hiroshima, Viet Nam.
    D. It was set of at noon on August 23, 1945, over the city of Hiroshima, Formosa.

2. Why did the atomic bomb take the inhabitants by surprise?
    A. They had been told the war was over.
    B. Only one plane was seen in the sky, and it was not thought of as dangerous.
    C. No one believed the United States had the scientific capability of building such a bomb.
    D. There had been so many recent scares and warning sirens that the people were starting to ignore them.

Hiroshima Multiple Choice Unit Test 2 Page 2

3. The survivors were amazed when they looked out over the city after the bomb. Why?
    A. The city was in much better shape physically than anyone had expected.
    B. There were no buildings standing.
    C. The entire city was on fire.
    D. Much of the city was giving off a thick, dreadful miasma.

4. Why were so many people burned?
    A. They suffered radiation burns.
    B. Many people were cooking over open fires when the bomb was dropped, and had kitchen fires.
    C. They were burned in the severe fires that started immediately after the explosion.
    D. Many people stayed outside to look at the damage, and were sunburned.

5. What were the estimated casualties just after the bomb hit?
    A. All but 50 people in the city were dead.
    B. Nearly 100,000 had been killed or doomed; 100,000 more were hurt.
    C. 200,000 were hurt, and 50,000 were dead.
    D. Half of the population, or 122,000 were either dead or wounded. The others were safe.

6. Where did the people go to be safe?
    A. They went to the mountains.
    B. They went to the park and to the river.
    C. They went to the hospital, which was still standing.
    D. They went into the underground shelters.

7. Why were the people nauseated?
    A. It was fear combined with exhaustion.
    B. They were hungry and ill from exposure to the elements.
    C. They were sick from the gas the Americans had dropped.
    D. They had radiation sickness, and had been drinking brackish water.

8. One of the survivors was rescuing wounded people. What did he have to keep reminding himself while he did so?
    A. He wanted to help all of the people, regardless of the clan they belonged to.
    B. He was helping human beings.
    C. They were probably contagious, and he should try to keep his nose and mouth covered.
    D. He tried to take the children and the elderly first.

Hiroshima Multiple Choice Unit Test 2 Page 3

9. Who was the doctor at the East Parade Ground taking care of first?
    A. He was taking care of the most seriously injured, to get them to perimeter hospitals and clear the area.
    B. He was taking care of the military personnel, so they could get back to work.
    C. He was taking care of the slightly wounded, in order to save as many lives as possible.
    D. He was taking care of children and pregnant women, because they had no one else to look after them.

10. What happened at two minutes after eleven o'clock on the morning of August 9th?
    A. A second atomic bomb was dropped on Nagasaki.
    B. The was a huge earthquake that leveled the city and killed most of the bomb survivors.
    C. The war was officially ended and peace was declared.
    D. Japan retaliated and bombed Pearl Harbor.

11. When Miss Sasaki saw the ruins of Hiroshima for the first time, what gave her the creeps?
    A. The city was deathly quiet.
    B. There were skeletons all over the streets, and they were giving off a yellow-green glow.
    C. There was a blanket of fresh, lush green, and wild flowers were blooming.
    D. Everything was dark. There was no electricity, and the sun was hidden by a covering of smoke and ash.

12. A few weeks to a month after the bomb people were having many symptoms. Which of the following is not one of the symptoms?
    A. Spot hemorrhages.
    B. Feelings of extreme weakness.
    C. Loss of hair.
    D. A wracking cough.

13. On September 17th, another disaster happened at Hiroshima. What was it?
    A. There was a 7.2 magnitude earthquake.
    B. There was an epidemic of smallpox.
    C. There was a cloudburst and a typhoon, which caused a flood.
    D. The people were so scared and frustrated that they began rioting in the streets. Many were killed and injured, and the rioting lasted far into the night.

Hiroshima Multiple Choice Unit Test 2 Page 4

14. What disease was becoming common among the survivors?
    A. It was hyperthyroidism.
    B. It was tuberculosis.
    C. It was leukemia.
    D. It was meningitis.

15. Why did the survivors suffer for more than a decade after the bombings?
    A. The government did not want to find itself saddled with anything like moral responsibility for the heinous acts of the victorious United States.
    B. The entire country was so depressed that no one could figure out what to do.
    C. Most of the doctors and nurses had died, and there was no one to work on finding a cure.
    D. The people were trying to show the rest of the world that they regretted the Japanese involvement in the war. They saw their suffering as a means of atonement for the sins of their leaders.

Hiroshima Multiple Choice Unit Test 2 Page 5

III. Composition

1. Choose any one of the six survivors written about in *Hiroshima* and tell his/her complete story in chronological order.

2. What is the message of the book *Hiroshima*? What should we get from reading it?

3. Explain why the bomb was dropped on Hiroshima.

Hiroshima Multiple Choice Unit Test 2 Page 6

IV. Vocabulary - Match the correct definitions to the words.

____ 1. APATHETIC		A. Those who teach Christian doctrines
____ 2. INTERMITTENT		B. Having a fear of foreigners
____ 3. TALISMANIC		C. Unpredictable
____ 4. CONTUSIONS		D. Book containing hymns and prayers
____ 5. REPUGNANT		E. Poisonous atmosphere
____ 6. CATECHIST		F. Return of a trait after a period of absence
____ 7. CAPRICIOUS		G. Represented or appearing as such
____ 8. CONSECRATE		H. Uncaring; uninterested
____ 9. EXTRICATED		I. Horrible; abominable; reprehensible
____ 10. SUCCINCT		J. Magical
____ 11. RECONNAISSANCE		K. Repulsive; disgusting; offensive
____ 12. SOLICITOUS		L. Bruises
____ 13. XENOPHOBIC		M. Japanese money
____ 14. MIASMA		N. Short and to the point
____ 15. HEINOUS		O. Make sacred
____ 16. YEN		P. Exploration of an area to gather information
____ 17. OSTENSIBLY		Q. Stopping and starting at intervals
____ 18. BUFFETED		R. Marked by anxious care and attentiveness
____ 19. ATAVISTIC		S. Forced; battered
____ 20. BREVIARY		T. Pulled out

ANSWER SHEET - *Hiroshima*
Multiple Choice Unit Tests

I. Matching
1. ___
2. ___
3. ___
4. ___
5. ___
6. ___
7. ___
8. ___
9. ___
10. ___

II. Multiple Choice
1. ___
2. ___
3. ___
4. ___
5. ___
6. ___
7. ___
8. ___
9. ___
10. ___
11. ___
12. ___
13. ___
14. ___
15. ___

IV. Vocabulary
1. ___
2. ___
3. ___
4. ___
5. ___
6. ___
7. ___
8. ___
9. ___
10. ___
11. ___
12. ___
13. ___
14. ___
15. ___
16. ___
17. ___
18. ___
19. ___
20. ___

ANSWER KEY - *Hiroshima*
Multiple Choice Unit Tests

Answers to Unit Test 1 are in the left column. Answers to Unit Test 2 are in the right column.

I. Matching	II. Multiple Choice	IV. Vocabulary
1. D G	1. B A	1. D H
2. G B	2. D B	2. L Q
3. B D	3. C D	3. F J
4. I E	4. C A	4. G L
5. H I	5. A B	5. P K
6. A C	6. D B	6. R A
7. E H	7. A D	7. B C
8. J F	8. C B	8. I O
9. C A	9. D C	9. C T
10. F J	10. D A	10. S N
	11. A C	11. N P
	12. B D	12. T R
	13. D B	13. J B
	14. B B	14. O E
	15. B A	15. H I
		16. E M
		17. K G
		18. M S
		19. Q F
		20. A D

UNIT RESOURCE MATERIALS

BULLETIN BOARD IDEAS - *Hiroshima*

1. Save one corner of the board for the best of students' *Hiroshima* writing assignments.

2. Take one of the word search puzzles from the extra activities section and with a marker copy it over in a large size on the bulletin board. Write the clue words to find to one side. Invite students prior to and after class to find the words and circle them on the bulletin board.

3. Write several of the most significant quotations from the book onto the board on brightly colored paper.

4. Make a bulletin board listing the vocabulary words for this unit. As you complete sections of the novel and discuss the vocabulary for each section, write the definitions on the bulletin board. (If your board is one students face frequently, it will help them learn the words.)

5. Place a map of Japan on the bulletin board. Put a star on Hiroshima. Cut out the names of the six survivors from the book and place them on either side of the map.

6. Make a travel bulletin board about Japan showing places of interest, geography, etc. (Your local travel agent should have lots of brochures and materials.)

7. Place a map of the world on the bulletin board and highlight Japan and the United States so students can see the physical relationship of the two countries.

8. Post recent articles about Japan and Japanese-American relations.

9. Many articles have been written about the bombing of Hiroshima and Nagasaki, especially with the 50th anniversary of the event being in 1995. Find some of these articles and post them on your bulletin board for students to read.

EXTRA ACTIVITIES - *Hiroshima*

One of the difficulties in teaching a novel is that all students don't read at the same speed. One student who likes to read may take the book home and finish it in a day or two. Sometimes a few students finish the in-class assignments early. The problem, then, is finding suitable extra activities for students.

One thing you can do is to keep a little library in the classroom. For this unit on *Hiroshima,* you might check out from the school library other related books and articles about Japan, World War II, atomic technology, the arms race, Japanese-Americans, Japanese-American relationships, careers in the military or in technology, etc.

Other things you may keep on hand are puzzles. WeI have made some relating directly to *Hiroshima* for you. Feel free to duplicate them.

Some students may like to draw. You might devise a contest or allow some extra-credit grade for students who draw characters or scenes from *Hiroshima*. Note, too, that if the students do not want to keep their drawings you may pick up some extra bulletin board materials this way. If you have a contest and you supply the prize (a CD or something like that perhaps), you could, possibly, make the drawing itself a non-refundable entry fee.

The pages which follow contain games, puzzles and worksheets. The keys, when appropriate, immediately follow the puzzle or worksheet. There are two main groups of activities: one group for the unit; that is, generally relating to the *Hiroshima* text, and another group of activities related strictly to the *Hiroshima* vocabulary.

Directions for these games, puzzles and worksheets are self-explanatory. The object here is to provide you with extra materials you may use in any way you choose.

MORE ACTIVITIES - *Hiroshima*

1. Pick a chapter or scene with a great deal of dialogue and have the students act it out on a stage. (Perhaps you could assign various scenes to different groups of students so more than one scene could be acted and more students could participate.)

2. Have students design a book cover (front and back and inside flaps) for *Hiroshima*.

3. Have students design a bulletin board (ready to be put up; not just sketched) for *Hiroshima*.

4. Have students plan a vacation in Japan: the cost, how to get there, where to stay, what to do, etc.

5. Have a Japanese "show and tell" day during which each student brings in something (or a picture of something) related to Japan and explains what it is and how it is related to Japan.

6. Have someone who knows Japanese come in and discuss the differences between Japanese language and writing and English language and writing. Have your guest explain why Japanese "sounds different" than European languages and how and why the writing is different.

7. Have a guest speaker come in to explain how a nuclear bomb and how nuclear energy work -- how so
    much destruction could have been caused by one bomb.

8. Have a panel of veterans discuss their involvement in and impressions from World War II, especially in the Pacific theater.

WORD SEARCH - *Hiroshima*

All words in this list are associated with *Hiroshima*. The words are placed backwards, forward, diagonally, up and down. The included words are listed below the word searches.

```
X K W N B H Q K Q G L D Y M L J F R K R M X Y D
W D A X J L E L Q N D J X N Z Z B S O J F Z N C
N P T M R R W R K U O F O Z W V F H G T W A V T
F U J I I K S A S A K I K A S A G A N A S A N O
N B N A N H G T T E T S S G T M T T L E G A N K
D S H A H S S D Z A Y A P O N R H E W X R L P M
V S P B B C L O I J L G M A L B I I R F S I G J
P A R K M R B D R G F I R E S P N C L E R K S K
J N I K N O A D O I C F G S R G X Q E O Z B J W
W K M M Y R B R C O H Y L H R I L E T N L K N H
R L L S E O T L U T L I M B T K C C R I V E R S
R C Z E S K A A L M G B B L R K O A F M B K V D
W K W J I T U Z N H A K X A F D W Y N P T C Y M
H K J J I N X E T I D K H K K Z M P J S P N N J
T Q K P P L S L L W M X A V H U R J N F V V D V
H G S S C M Y O P Z J O J N L D S S K Y B T T B
K O Q W W F L M R C Y V T K Q L X H Z G S Z F M
H T B K S W T R D G Y T X O G L R M A Q B D F K
W R W Y W W V Z B E K X G Y J N W M P W M J T
C M V W Q R L Q R P X Y T Q H S J D T P V J B J
```

AMERICANS	FIRES	LEUKEMIA	RIVERS
ASANO	FUJII	LIGHT	SASAKI
ATOMIC	HAIR	MRB	SASKI
BLOOD	HERSEY	NAGASAKI	SEWING
BOMB	HIBAKUSHA	NAKAMURA	SIREN
CLERK	HIROSHIMA	NUN	SLIGHTLY
DOCTOR	HOSPITAL	PARK	SPAS
DUST	JAPAN	PASTOR	TANIMOTO
EXPLOSION	KLEINSORGE	RADIATION	WATER
FAN	KYO	RICE	

KEY: WORD SEARCH - *Hiroshima*

All words in this list are associated with *Hiroshima*. The words are placed backwards, forward, diagonally, up and down. The included words are listed below the word searches.

```
                H                               R
        A       E       N D       N             O   F
    N   M   R   R   U O   O   W               T   A
F U J I I K S A S A K I K A S A G A N A S A N O
    N A N H   T   E T S S   T   T       E   A
    H A     S     A Y A P   R   E W     R   P
    P B       O I   L   M A L   I I R       I
P A R K M R B D R   F I R E S P N C L E R K S
J   I K   O A   O I C   G S R G X     E O
    K   M Y R B R   O H   L H   I   E T
      L   E O T L U   L I       T   C C R I V E R S
        E   K A A   M G B B         O A
          I T U   N H A     A   D       N
          I N   E T I   K       K       S
            P     S L L   M   A       U
        S       Y O       O   N     S
      O           R       T         H
    H                 G       O       A
                        E
```

AMERICANS	FIRES	LEUKEMIA	RIVERS
ASANO	FUJII	LIGHT	SASAKI
ATOMIC	HAIR	MRB	SASKI
BLOOD	HERSEY	NAGASAKI	SEWING
BOMB	HIBAKUSHA	NAKAMURA	SIREN
CLERK	HIROSHIMA	NUN	SLIGHTLY
DOCTOR	HOSPITAL	PARK	SPAS
DUST	JAPAN	PASTOR	TANIMOTO
EXPLOSION	KLEINSORGE	RADIATION	WATER
FAN	KYO	RICE	

CROSSWORD - *Hiroshima*

CROSSWORD CLUES - *Hiroshima*

ACROSS

1. German priest
4. The one after
5. These disorders are common in the second stages of radiation sickness
7. Negative reply
8. Saski's occupation
10. Shape of the city of Hiroshima
11. Initials for the United States
12. Nickname for the B29 bombers
14. Kind of bombs dropped on Japan
15. Blood disease common among survivors
18. They dropped the bombs
20. Country in which Hiroshima is located
22. Clerk at East Asia Tin Works trapped under bookcases
23. Unusual
26. Coordinating conjunction; also
27. Sasaki built these
28. City on which 2nd bomb was dropped
29. People saw a bright ___ when the bomb went off
31. Mrs. Nakamura's ___ machine rusted in her well
34. Belonging to me
35. Fujii's occupation
36. Portion allotted during a shortage
37. Make up for
39. Waterways of Hiroshima

DOWN

1. River near Asano Park
2. Saski eventually became one
3. Food
4. Tailor's widow with small children
5. Two were dropped on Japan
6. Kind of cloud in Hiroshima after the bomb
9. There was no sound of an ___ when the bomb went off
10. The bombs caused these & winds blew them out of control
13. Explosion-affected persons
14. ___ Park
16. Doctor who owned & operated a private hospital
17. One symptom of radiation sickness; ___ falls out
19. People suffered from ___ sickness & burns
21. Asano ___
22. Doctor at Red Cross hospital; became wealthy
24. Tanimoto's occupation
25. Pastor of Hiroshima Methodist Church
26. Help
29. When Japanese ___ed at radar, they only saw one plane
30. Acquire
31. Warning sound telling people to go to safe areas
32. People drank contaminated ___
33. Shooting weapon
38. Either's partner

CROSSWORD ANSWER KEY - *Hiroshima*

MATCHING/QUIZ WORKSHEET 1 - *Hiroshima*

____ 1. NAGASAKI   A. They dropped the bombs

____ 2. HIROSHIMA   B. People drank contaminated ___

____ 3. SASKI   C. Tailor's widow with small children

____ 4. AMERICANS   D. Sasaki built these

____ 5. HAIR   E. Author

____ 6. FUJII   F. The bombs caused these & winds blew them out of control

____ 7. EXPLOSION   G. Blood disease common among survivors

____ 8. TANIMOTO   H. People suffered from ___ sickness & burns

____ 9. KYO   I. Short-staffed, over-crowded places after the bombing

____ 10. WATER   J. One symptom of radiation sickness; ___ falls out

____ 11. SPAS   K. There was no sound of an ___ when the bomb went off

____ 12. RADIATION   L. Doctor who owned & operated a private hospital

____ 13. MRB   M. City on which 2nd bomb was dropped

____ 14. HOSPITAL   N. Explosion-affected persons

____ 15. LEUKEMIA   O. Pastor of Hiroshima Methodist Church

____ 16. HERSEY   P. Nickname for the B29 bombers

____ 17. NAKAMURA   Q. Clerk at East Asia Tin Works trapped under bookcases

____ 18. DOCTOR   R. River near Asano Park

____ 19. FIRES   S. Fujii's occupation

____ 20. HIBAKUSHA   T. City on which 1st bomb was dropped

KEY: MATCHING/QUIZ WORKSHEET 1 - *Hiroshima*

_M_	1. NAGASAKI	A.	They dropped the bombs
_T_	2. HIROSHIMA	B.	People drank contaminated ___
_Q_	3. SASKI	C.	Tailor's widow with small children
_A_	4. AMERICANS	D.	Sasaki built these
_J_	5. HAIR	E.	Author
_L_	6. FUJII	F.	The bombs caused these & winds blew them out of control
_K_	7. EXPLOSION	G.	Blood disease common among survivors
_O_	8. TANIMOTO	H.	People suffered from ___ sickness & burns
_R_	9. KYO	I.	Short-staffed, over-crowded places after the bombing
_B_	10. WATER	J.	One symptom of radiation sickness; ___ falls out
_D_	11. SPAS	K	There was no sound of an ___ when the bomb went off
_H_	12. RADIATION	L.	Doctor who owned & operated a private hospital
_P_	13. MRB	M.	City on which 2nd bomb was dropped
_I_	14. HOSPITAL	N.	Explosion-affected persons
_G_	15. LEUKEMIA	O.	Pastor of Hiroshima Methodist Church
_E_	16. HERSEY	P.	Nickname for the B29 bombers
_C_	17. NAKAMURA	Q.	Clerk at East Asia Tin Works trapped under bookcases
_S_	18. DOCTOR	R.	River near Asano Park
_F_	19. FIRES	S.	Fujii's occupation
_N_	20. HIBAKUSHA	T.	City on which 1st bomb was dropped

MATCHING/QUIZ WORKSHEET 2 - *Hiroshima*

____ 1. KYO   A. Nickname for the B29 bombers

____ 2. BOMB   B. Two were dropped on Japan

____ 3. DUST   C. Tailor's widow with small children

____ 4. ATOMIC   D. Kind of cloud in Hiroshima after the bomb

____ 5. HOSPITAL   E. Asano ___

____ 6. FIRES   F. Waterways of Hiroshima

____ 7. ASANO   G. Fujii's occupation

____ 8. PASTOR   H. Tanimoto's occupation

____ 9. NAKAMURA   I. The bombs caused these & winds blew them out of control

____ 10. RIVERS   J. Food

____ 11. LIGHT   K. ___ Park

____ 12. HIBAKUSHA L. Explosion-affected persons

____ 13. SASAKI   M. Short-staffed, over-crowded places after the bombing

____ 14. HIROSHIMA N. City on which 1st bomb was dropped

____ 15. DOCTOR   O. They dropped the bombs

____ 16. MRB   P. People saw a bright ___ when the bomb went off

____ 17. RICE   Q. People drank contaminated ___

____ 18. PARK   R. Doctor at Red Cross hospital; became wealthy

____ 19. AMERICANS S. Kind of bombs dropped on Japan

____ 20. WATER   T. River near Asano Park

KEY: MATCHING/QUIZ WORKSHEET 2 - *Hiroshima*

_T_	1. KYO	A. Nickname for the B29 bombers
_B_	2. BOMB	B. Two were dropped on Japan
_D_	3. DUST	C. Tailor's widow with small children
_S_	4. ATOMIC	D. Kind of cloud in Hiroshima after the bomb
_M_	5. HOSPITAL	E. Asano ___
_I_	6. FIRES	F. Waterways of Hiroshima
_K_	7. ASANO	G. Fujii's occupation
_H_	8. PASTOR	H. Tanimoto's occupation
_C_	9. NAKAMURA	I. The bombs caused these & winds blew them out of control
_F_	10. RIVERS	J. Food
_P_	11. LIGHT	K. ___ Park
_L_	12. HIBAKUSHA	L. Explosion-affected persons
_R_	13. SASAKI	M. Short-staffed, over-crowded places after the bombing
_N_	14. HIROSHIMA	N. City on which 1st bomb was dropped
_G_	15. DOCTOR	O. They dropped the bombs
_A_	16. MRB	P. People saw a bright ___ when the bomb went off
_J_	17. RICE	Q. People drank contaminated ___
_E_	18. PARK	R. Doctor at Red Cross hospital; became wealthy
_O_	19. AMERICANS	S. Kind of bombs dropped on Japan
_Q_	20. WATER	T. River near Asano Park

JUGGLE LETTER REVIEW GAME CLUE SHEET - *Hiroshima*

SCRAMBLED	WORD	CLUE
RAMINACES	AMERICANS	They dropped the bombs
NASOA	ASANO	___ Park
MOTICA	ATOMIC	Kind of bombs dropped on Japan
OLOBD	BLOOD	These disorders are common in the second stages of radiation sickness
MOBB	BOMB	Two were dropped on Japan
RKLEC	CLERK	Saski's occupation
DROOTC	DOCTOR	Fujii's occupation
STUD	DUST	Kind of cloud in Hiroshima after the bomb
SLOOPNEXI	EXPLOSION	There was no sound of an ___ when the bomb went off
NAF	FAN	Shape of the city of Hiroshima
SIREF	FIRES	The bombs caused these & winds blew them out of control
IJUFI	FUJII	Doctor who owned & operated a private hospital
RHAI	HAIR	One symptom of radiation sickness; ___ falls out
SHEERY	HERSEY	Author
KABHUISAH	HIBAKUSHA	Explosion-affected persons
MORIHASH	HIROSHIMA	City on which 1st bomb was dropped
SLOPTHIA	HOSPITAL	Short-staffed, over-crowded places after the bombing
ANJPA	JAPAN	Country in which Hiroshima is located
NEKGOLSIRE	KLEINSORGE	German priest
YOK	KYO	River near Asano Park
MEEKAULI	LEUKEMIA	Blood disease common among survivors
THILG	LIGHT	People saw a bright ___ when the bomb went off
BRM	MRB	Nickname for the B29 bombers
ANKASIGA	NAGASAKI	City on which 2nd bomb was dropped
KUNMRAAA	NAKAMURA	Tailor's widow with small children
UNN	NUN	Saski eventually became one
KRAP	PARK	Asano ___
TORPSA	PASTOR	Tanimoto's occupation
ITODAIRNA	RADIATION	People suffered from ___ sickness & burns
CIRE	RICE	Food
VSERRI	RIVERS	Waterways of Hiroshima
SKAAIS	SASAKI	Doctor at Red Cross hospital; became wealthy
KISSA	SASKI	Clerk at East Asia Tin Works trapped under bookcases
GINEWS	SEWING	Mrs. Nakamura's ___ machine rusted in her well
INRES	SIREN	Warning sound telling people to go to safe areas
YTHILSLG	SLIGHTLY	East Parade Ground doctor's first duty was to take care of the ___ wounded
PASS	SPAS	Sasaki built these

VOCABULARY RESOURCE MATERIALS

VOCABULARY WORD SEARCH - *Hiroshima*

All words in this list are associated with *Hiroshima* with an emphasis on the vocabulary words chosen for study in the text. The words are placed backwards, forward, diagonally, up and down. The included words are listed below.

```
C L H D S F G E S Y D T D C S R B K Y K T V N S
M O R I B U N D C A T E C H I S T U P E F I E D
S R N Y H J T H R N C H T N P N Y M F Q N D D H
L G B T Y V A N Y R A I P A I O A B I F Y B T K
C R U X U R J P E G P S T A R C M M A A E L N M
X O Q X R S A P R T C U S E R U C M S R S T T Z
N R N E W K I I B E T O T I H O P U E I I M E Z
H N D S C T N O D R C I N R A T X P S L L T A D
S E O E E A H E N N E A M V E N A Y U P E A E P
G N D I T C P E F S E V R R I S N P S S T D T S
M Y O O T A R R I F R C I I E V C O A M X J D V
F C L I N I C A I N I E N A O T I E C J S B C M
G C W B T I L I T C O C P I R U N A N E T C Y N
R Y K W I A S O R E I U A U R Y S I L C R L Z P
W S K T M S N T V T R O S C G Q J J P D E N K L
D Q J D F H N A I F X G U M I N R Q G T K N L Y
P X H H F P R E M C S E J S X O A Y C D X G Q K
M X V Z T T H V T E R W K B C R U N M X F S F M
S O L I C I T O U S K V A T A V I S T I C P M P
X E N O P H O B I C O R U D I M E N T A R Y H Z
```

APATHETIC	CONVIVIAL	MALAISE	RUDIMENTARY
ATAVISTIC	CRUX	MIASMA	SOLICITOUS
BREVIARY	DECREPIT	MORIBUND	STUPEFIED
BUFFETED	EFFICACIOUS	OSTENSIBLY	SUCCINCT
CAPRICIOUS	EMANATIONS	PAROXYSM	SUPPURATED
CATECHIST	EXTRICATED	PUMMELED	SYBARITES
CHAGRIN	HEDONISTIC	PRECARIOUS	TALISMANIC
CHARRED	HEINOUS	PUTRESCENCE	VOLITION
CONSECRATE	INCENDIARY	RECONNAISSANCE	XENOPHOBIC
CONTUSIONS	INTERMITTENT	REPUGNANT	YEN

KEY: VOCABULARY WORD SEARCH - *Hiroshima*

All words in this list are associated with *Hiroshima* with an emphasis on the vocabulary words chosen for study in the text. The words are placed backwards, forward, diagonally, up and down. The included words are listed below.

```
        C               E       D T D C       B   Y
        M O R I B U N D C A T E C H I S T U P E F I E D
            N           T H   N C H T N P N Y M F   N
              T Y     A N   R A I P A I O A B I F
        C R U X U R     P E G P S T A R C M M A A E
            O       R S A P R T C U S E R U C M S R S T
            N E       I I B E T O T I H O P U E I I M E
        H N D S C T N O D R C I N R A T X P S L L T A D
        S E O E E A H E N N E A M V E N A Y U   E A E
            N D I T C P E F S E V R R I S N P S S   D T S
            Y O O T A R R I F R C I I E V C O A M
              L I N I C A I N I E N A O T I E C
                B T I L I T C O C P I R U N A N E
                I A S O R E I U A U   Y S I L C R
                  M S N T V T   O S C G           E
                    N A I   X   U   I N
                      E M C   E   S   O A
                        T E             U N
        S O L I C I T O U S     A T A V I S T I C
        X E N O P H O B I C O R U D I M E N T A R Y
```

APATHETIC	CONVIVIAL	MALAISE	RUDIMENTARY
ATAVISTIC	CRUX	MIASMA	SOLICITOUS
BREVIARY	DECREPIT	MORIBUND	STUPEFIED
BUFFETED	EFFICACIOUS	OSTENSIBLY	SUCCINCT
CAPRICIOUS	EMANATIONS	PAROXYSM	SUPPURATED
CATECHIST	EXTRICATED	PUMMELED	SYBARITES
CHAGRIN	HEDONISTIC	PRECARIOUS	TALISMANIC
CHARRED	HEINOUS	PUTRESCENCE	VOLITION
CONSECRATE	INCENDIARY	RECONNAISSANCE	XENOPHOBIC
CONTUSIONS	INTERMITTENT	REPUGNANT	YEN

VOCABULARY CROSSWORD - *Hiroshima*

VOCABULARY CROSSWORD CLUES - *Hiroshima*

ACROSS
3. About to die
7. Feeling of embarrassment or humiliation caused by failure or disappointment
11. Short and to the point
12. Ingested food
13. Pulled out
14. Food
15. Unpredictable
21. Prefix meaning small
22. Saski eventually became one
23. People saw a bright ___ when the bomb went off
24. A sign of radiation sickness is hair falling ___
25. Tanimoto's occupation
27. Japanese money
28. America dropped a bomb -- Hiroshima
29. River near Asano Park
30. Book containing hymns and prayers
33. Nickname for the B29 bombers
34. Kind of bombs dropped on Japan
35. Two were dropped on Japan
38. Through 6 people, Hersey gives us different ---- of the Hiroshima story
40. Something that comes forth from a source
42. Fujii's occupation
44. Assuming a false attitude; posturing
47. Horrible; abominable; reprehensible
48. These disorders are common in the second stages of radiation sickness
49. Asano ___
50. Uncaring; uninterested

DOWN
1. Shape of the city of Hiroshima
2. Basic, central or critical point
3. Sense of bodily discomfort, depression or unease
4. City public transportation
5. Worn out; broken down from use
6. Bruises
7. Those who teach Christian doctrines
8. Neither's partner
9. Return of a trait after a period of absence
10. Characterized by the pursuit of sensual pleasure
16. Sudden outburst
17. Make sacred
18. Possess
19. There was no sound of an __ when the bomb went off
20. Scorched
26. The bombs caused these & winds blew them out of control
31. Sociable
32. Warning sound telling people to go to safe areas
36. Person under a doctor's care
37. ___ Park
39. Injuries, especially those with broken skin
41. Poisonous atmosphere
43. Saski's occupation
45. Kind of cloud in Hiroshima after the bomb
46. Opposite of bad

VOCABULARY CROSSWORD ANSWER KEY - *Hiroshima*

			F		C					M	O	R	I	B	U	N	D		C		
		C	H	A	G	R	I	N		A				U		E		O		A
		A		N		U		O		L		H		S	U	C	C	I	N	C	T
	A	T	E		E	X	T	R	I	C	A	T	E	D		R		T		A
		E						I		D		R	I	C	E		U		V
		C	A	P	R	I	C	I	O	U	S					P		S		I
E		H		A		O		W		E	N		C		M	I	N	I		S
X		I		R		N	U	N			L	I	G	H	T		T		O	U	T
P	A	S	T	O	R		S		F		S		A					N		I
L		T		X		Y	E	N		I		T		R				S		C
O	N		K	Y	O		C		B	R	E	V	I	A	R	Y		C		S
S			S		M	R	B		E			C	E		A	T	O	M	I	C
I		B	O	M	B		A		S				D				N		R
O					T		P						A			V	I	E	W	S
N			W	E	M	A	N	A	T	I	O	N	S			I		N	
	D	O	C	T	O	R		I		T			A			V			
		L		U		A	T	T	I	T	U	D	I	N	I	Z	I	N	G
	H	E	I	N	O	U	S		E		U		O			A		O
		R		D		M		N		S			B	L	O	O	D
P	A	R	K	S		A	P	A	T	H	E	T	I	C			D

VOCABULARY WORKSHEET 1 - *Hiroshima*

____ 1. Beat; hit
    A. Breviary   B. Pummeled   C. Prefectural   D. Apathetic

____ 2. Stopping and starting at intervals
    A. Putrescence   B. Yen   C. Extricated   D. Intermittent

____ 3. Scorched
    A. Putrescence   B. Crux   C. Chagrin   D. Charred

____ 4. Bruises
    A. Charred   B. Volition   C. Contusions   D. Breviary

____ 5. Basic, central or critical point
    A. Crux   B. Stupefied   C. Succinct   D. Incendiary

____ 6. Unpredictable
    A. Convivial   B. Attitudinizing   C. Capricious   D. Emanations

____ 7. Dangerously lacking in security or stability
    A. Catechist   B. Buffeted   C. Volition   D. Precarious

____ 8. Japanese money
    A. Repugnant   B. Yen   C. Hedonistic   D. Moribund

____ 9. Sociable
    A. Sybarites   B. Apathetic   C. Hedonistic   D. Convivial

____ 10. Book containing hymns and prayers
    A. Malaise   B. Breviary   C. Charred   D. Sybarites

____ 11. Pulled out
    A. Volition   B. Extricated   C. Ostensibly   D. Decrepit

____ 12. Make sacred
    A. Heinous   B. Paroxysm   C. Talismanic   D. Consecrate

____ 13. Of or containing chemicals that cause fire when exploded
    A. Precarious   B. Incendiary   C. Repugnant   D. Convivial

____ 14. Characterized by the pursuit of sensual pleasure
    A. Xenophobic   B. Hedonistic   C. Moribund   D. Decrepit

____ 15. Poisonous atmosphere
    A. Rudimentary   B. Solicitous   C. Miasma   D. Crux

____ 16. Those who teach Christian doctrines
    A. Catechist   B. Reconnaissance   C. Xenophobic   D. Contusions

____ 17. Decomposed, rotten, foul-smelling matter
    A. Capricious   B. Putrescence   C. Apathetic   D. Consecrate

____ 18. Conscious decision
    A. Breviary   B. Incendiary   C. Reconnaissance   D. Volition

____ 19. Feeling of embarrassment or humiliation caused by failure or disappointment
    A. Reconnaissance   B. Chagrin   C. Talismanic   D. Efficacious

____ 20. Repulsive; disgusting; offensive
    A. Repugnant   B. Extricated   C. Ostensibly   D. Apathetic

KEY: VOCABULARY WORKSHEET 1 - *Hiroshima*

_B_ 1. Beat; hit
    A. Breviary   B. Pommeled   C. Prefectural   D. Apathetic

_D_ 2. Stopping and starting at intervals
    A. Putrescence   B. Yen   C. Extricated   D. Intermittent

_D_ 3. Scorched
    A. Putrescence   B. Crux   C. Chagrin   D. Charred

_C_ 4. Bruises
    A. Charred   B. Volition   C. Contusions   D. Breviary

_A_ 5. Basic, central or critical point
    A. Crux   B. Stupefied   C. Succinct   D. Incendiary

_C_ 6. Unpredictable
    A. Convivial   B. Attitudinizing   C. Capricious   D. Emanations

_D_ 7. Dangerously lacking in security or stability
    A. Catechist   B. Buffeted   C. Volition   D. Precarious

_B_ 8. Japanese money
    A. Repugnant   B. Yen   C. Hedonistic   D. Moribund

_D_ 9. Sociable
    A. Sybarites   B. Apathetic   C. Hedonistic   D. Convivial

_B_ 10. Book containing hymns and prayers
    A. Malaise   B. Breviary   C. Charred   D. Sybarites

_B_ 11. Pulled out
    A. Volition   B. Extricated   C. Ostensibly   D. Decrepit

_D_ 12. Make sacred
    A. Heinous   B. Paroxysm   C. Talismanic   D. Consecrate

_B_ 13. Of or containing chemicals that cause fire when exploded
    A. Precarious   B. Incendiary   C. Repugnant   D. Convivial

_B_ 14. Characterized by the pursuit of sensual pleasure
    A. Xenophobic   B. Hedonistic   C. Moribund   D. Decrepit

_C_ 15. Poisonous atmosphere
    A. Rudimentary   B. Solicitous   C. Miasma   D. Crux

_A_ 16. Those who teach Christian doctrines
    A. Catechist   B. Reconnaissance   C. Xenophobic   D. Contusions

_B_ 17. Decomposed, rotten, foul-smelling matter
    A. Capricious   B. Putrescence   C. Apathetic   D. Consecrate

_D_ 18. Conscious decision
    A. Breviary   B. Incendiary   C. Reconnaissance   D. Volition

_B_ 19. Feeling of embarrassment or humiliation caused by failure or disappointment
    A. Reconnaissance   B. Chagrin   C. Talismanic   D. Efficacious

_A_ 20. Repulsive; disgusting; offensive
    A. Repugnant   B. Extricated   C. Ostensibly   D. Apathetic

VOCABULARY WORKSHEET 2 - *Hiroshima*

____ 1. BREVIARY	A. Something that comes forth from a source

____ 2. CHAGRIN	B. Horrible; abominable; reprehensible

____ 3. MORIBUND	C. Forced; battered

____ 4. EFFICACIOUS	D. Conscious decision

____ 5. SOLICITOUS	E. Worn out; broken down from use

____ 6. PUMMELED	F. Sudden outburst

____ 7. BUFFETED	G. Book containing hymns and prayers

____ 8. TALISMANIC	H. Stopping and starting at intervals

____ 9. ATAVISTIC	I. About to die

____ 10. OSTENSIBLY	J. Of or containing chemicals that cause fire when exploded

____ 11. DECREPIT	K. Represented or appearing as such

____ 12. EMANATIONS	L. Marked by anxious care and attentiveness

____ 13. VOLITION	M. Sociable

____ 14. CONVIVIAL	N. Producing the desired effect

____ 15. HEDONISTIC	O. Magical

____ 16. PAROXYSM	P. Characterized by the pursuit of sensual pleasure

____ 17. HEINOUS	Q. Beat; hit

____ 18. INCENDIARY	R. Return of a trait after a period of absence

____ 19. INTERMITTENT	S. Basic, central or critical point

____ 20. CRUX	T. Feeling of embarrassment or humiliation caused by failure or disappointment

KEY: VOCABULARY WORKSHEET 2 - *Hiroshima*

_G_	1. BREVIARY	A.	Something that comes forth from a source
_T_	2. CHAGRIN	B.	Horrible; abominable; reprehensible
_I_	3. MORIBUND	C.	Forced; battered
_N_	4. EFFICACIOUS	D.	Conscious decision
_L_	5. SOLICITOUS	E.	Worn out; broken down from use
_Q_	6. POMMELED	F.	Sudden outburst
_C_	7. BUFFETED	G.	Book containing hymns and prayers
_O_	8. TALISMANIC	H.	Stopping and starting at intervals
_R_	9. ATAVISTIC	I.	About to die
_K_	10. OSTENSIBLY	J.	Of or containing chemicals that cause fire when exploded
_E_	11. DECREPIT	K.	Represented or appearing as such
_A_	12. EMANATIONS	L.	Marked by anxious care and attentiveness
_D_	13. VOLITION	M.	Sociable
_M_	14. CONVIVIAL	N.	Producing the desired effect
_P_	15. HEDONISTIC	O.	Magical
_F_	16. PAROXYSM	P.	Characterized by the pursuit of sensual pleasure
_B_	17. HEINOUS	Q.	Beat; hit
_J_	18. INCENDIARY	R.	Return of a trait after a period of absence
_H_	19. INTERMITTENT	S.	Basic, central or critical point
_S_	20. CRUX	T.	Feeling of embarrassment or humiliation caused by failure or disappointment

VOCABULARY JUGGLE LETTER REVIEW GAME CLUES - *Hiroshima*

SCRAMBLED	WORD	CLUE
INLOVITO	VOLITION	Conscious decision
NOINSECANSCARE	RECONNAISSANCE	Exploration of an area to gather information
TINTERTIMTEN	INTERMITTENT	Stopping and starting at intervals
NIDCAYRENI	INCENDIARY	Of or containing chemicals that cause fire when exploded
MEELPLODM	POMMELED	Beat; hit
SHEDONICIT	HEDONISTIC	Characterized by the pursuit of sensual pleasure
VOLIVINAC	CONVIVIAL	Sociable
POBINEXHOC	XENOPHOBIC	Having a fear of foreigners
UNPERTANG	REPUGNANT	Repulsive; disgusting; offensive
SUTILSOOIC	SOLICITOUS	Marked by anxious care and attentiveness
SIAMMA	MIASMA	Poisonous atmosphere
THEACSTIC	CATECHIST	Those who teach Christian doctrines
VERYRIBA	BREVIARY	Book containing hymns and prayers
CITEXDTEAR	EXTRICATED	Pulled out
CHATETPIA	APATHETIC	Uncaring; uninterested
OXYPRAMS	PAROXYSM	Sudden outburst
ASTIVICTA	ATAVISTIC	Return of a trait after a period of absence
UPPERDAUST	SUPPURATED	Full of pus
ONUSITSONC	CONTUSIONS	Bruises
TCUCSINC	SUCCINCT	Short and to the point
LAFETREPURC	PREFECTURAL	District administered or governed by a prefect
TUFEEDSPI	STUPEFIED	With senses dulled by amazement
HARCRED	CHARRED	Scorched
TUSNERPECCE	PUTRESCENCE	Decomposed, rotten, foul-smelling matter
BIMRUDNO	MORIBUND	About to die
AMISNALTIC	TALISMANIC	Magical
NYE	YEN	Japanese money
DRITPEEC	DECREPIT	Worn out; broken down from use
FUDBETEF	BUFFETED	Forced; battered
SALAMIE	MALAISE	Sense of bodily discomfort, depression or unease
APRISCOUCI	CAPRICIOUS	Unpredictable
SITONAMNAE	EMANATIONS	Something that comes forth from a source
TRACONSECE	CONSECRATE	Make sacred
CXRU	CRUX	Basic, central or critical point
REAROSICUP	PRECARIOUS	Dangerously lacking in security or stability
OSHEINU	HEINOUS	Horrible; abominable; reprehensible
TTTIIIDIAGUNZN	ATTITUDINIZING	Assuming a false attitude; posturing
ISCAFFEICOU	EFFICACIOUS	Producing the desired effect
BSNETOSLYI	OSTENSIBLY	Represented or appearing as such

www.ingramcontent.com/pod-product-compliance
Lightning Source LLC
Chambersburg PA
CBHW051416070526
44584CB00023B/3454